I0970364

THE
ART OF
WINNING
Foundation
Grants

THE ART OF WINNING

Foundation Grants

BY HOWARD HILLMAN AND

KARIN ABARBANEL

THE VANGUARD PRESS, INC. NEW YORK

Library of Congress Catalogue Card Number: 75–387
ISBN 0–8149–0759–8
Designer: Ernst Reichl
Manufactured in the United States of America
Second Printing

*This book is dedicated to
the hundreds of thousands of grant-seekers
who, through trial and error,
have collectively developed
the art of winning
foundation grants.*

CONTENTS

8

Part Four: Sample Proposal 155

PREFACE

Grant-making is big business. This year America's 25,000 foundations will award some 400,000 grants totaling roughly $2 billion.

These statistics may lead some to think that foundation dollars are growing on trees just waiting to be picked. Not so. Over 95 out of every 100 grant applications are turned down.

But don't let this 95 percent rejection rate discourage you. Many of these rejections would not have occurred if the grant-seekers had known the basic principles learned by previous grant-seekers through trial and error.

This book outlines those principles in an easy-to-follow, step-by-step approach. While we can't guarantee you success, we believe that if you study the steps carefully, the odds of your winning a grant will be significantly improved.

THE
ART OF
WINNING
Foundation
Grants

PART ONE
Ten Steps to Success

INTRODUCTION
TO PART ONE

No two grant-seekers use exactly the same approach in their quests for foundation funds—and each individual grant-seeker varies the approach from project to project.

However, some guidelines are necessary. We therefore give you the ten steps generally employed by the majority of experienced grant-seekers:

STEP 1   Define Your Goal
STEP 2   Assess Your Chances
STEP 3   Organize Your Resources
STEP 4   Identify Your Prospects
STEP 5   Research Your Prospects in Depth
STEP 6   Make Your Initial Contact
STEP 7   Meet With the Foundation
STEP 8   Write Your Formal Proposal
STEP 9   Submit Your Formal Proposal
STEP 10 Follow-up

Carefully study the "consensus" approach described in the ensuing pages, then adapt it to fit the project at hand. For example, if you are fortunate enough to know ahead of time the names of all your most promising foundation prospects, then you would skip Step 4.

How long does it take, if you're successful, to proceed from Step 1 to that joyous moment when the check arrives in the mail? In almost all instances the time span is long:

six months if you're lucky, but more likely one year and sometimes longer.

What makes a successful grant-seeker? To find the elusive answer we sought a consensus of professionals in the field. Besides experience, here are the seven most mentioned qualities: SALESMANSHIP—To win a grant one must sell ideas to other people. COMMUNICATIONS SKILLS —One must know how to write and speak effectively. INGENUITY and FLEXIBILITY—One seldom follows the same path twice. RESEARCH SKILLS—One must know the tools and how to use them. ADMINISTRATIVE SKILLS—One must possess the full spectrum, from accounting to leadership. GOOD HUMAN RELATIONS—One must constantly motivate and gain the cooperation of many people beyond the immediate staff: other departments, community leaders, and foundation officials.

The seventh quality is PERSISTENCE AND DEDICATION— Grant-seeking takes time and is seldom easy.

STEP 1

Define Your Goal

Successful grant-seeking depends largely upon finding those foundations whose goals match the goals of your project. Unless you have your goal well defined, you are seriously handicapped from the very beginning in your pursuit of foundation funds.

A good test of a clearly defined goal is whether it can be stated in no more than a brief paragraph or two. Longer definitions usually indicate less than precise thinking.

To help you pinpoint your goal, use these questions experienced grant-seekers ask themselves:

What is the need? Its significance and scope?
What are others doing to solve the need?
What aspects of the overall problem can our organization as the grant-seeker realistically attempt to solve? In the short term? In the long term?
Who is the target population in terms of:
    Size?
    Geographical scope?
    Socio-economic background?
    Other vital statistics?
Can the benefits to the target population be measured?
Is solving the need a priority within our organization? Within our community?

Some of the above questions are similar to ones that foundations ask themselves when evaluating proposals. A complete list of those questions is found in Step 2.

Put the definition of your goal down on paper, even if only in rough-draft form. Writing helps you to clarify your thoughts. Double-check your definition's practicality and wording by showing it to others in your organization and field. Often they can point out your blind spots.

STEP 2

Assess Your Chances

With your goal at least roughly defined you are in a position to take the step most often overlooked by grant-seekers: objectively assessing your chances of success.

It makes little economic sense to implement a grant-seeking campaign unless the return justifies the investment. Grant-seeking endeavors, at least successful ones, usually require a substantial outlay of money and time, especially the latter. Step 2 is designed to help you determine early if foundations are a viable source of funds for you.

You'll have a difficult time winning a foundation grant if:

You Don't Have an Internal Revenue Service (IRS) Letter of Exemption—Foundations by law can fund only certain types of activities. If we may simplify, these fundable activities are: charitable, educational, religious, scientific, and cultural. Foundations can legally award grants to an organization performing one of these activities, whether or not that organization has an IRS Letter of Exemption. Foundations can also make grants to individuals. However, these facts can be misleading to a potential grant-seeker. In actual practice, foundations give virtually all their money to organizations with the IRS tax-exempt status.

The prime reason for this grant-making policy is a foundation's fear of stiff IRS penalties for giving money to ineligible recipients. By funding a recipient with the IRS Letter of Exemption, a foundation feels secure because that document is quasi-governmental approval of the recipient's eligibility. Without this document it is difficult and sometimes costly for a foundation to determine whether the grant-applicant is legally eligible. As a result, foundations play it safe by primarily funding organizations with tax-exempt status.

For details on how to apply for tax-exempt status see Appendix F.

If your tax-exempt application is not approved, or if you cannot afford to wait, or if you can't get the approval in the first place because you are an individual, then you have an alternative. You can scout around for an existing tax-exempt organization willing to sponsor your project. The foundation check would be sent to your sponsor, who would turn the money over to you. Usually, the sponsor deducts about 5 percent to 10 percent to cover administrative expenses. (Record these dollars in your budget.)

Your organization is politically oriented—The Tax Reform Act of 1969 prohibits a foundation from giving money to organizations involved in any type of political activity. This restriction includes disseminating information that might influence a vote, whether it be a Senator's or John Q. Public's.

Your field is not well funded—Foundations have historically funded some fields more than others. To determine the fundability of your field, examine "The Most-Funded Fields," Appendix B. Keep in mind, however, that this data is categorized into fields that might not coincide with the name of your field. For example, if you are a producer of film documentaries and desire to make a film on nursing, you would look in Appendix B under "Health: Nursing," not under "Film." Some fields are especially well funded. But don't assume that this fact makes it easier to secure a grant. Competition for financial assistance in these well-funded fields generally increases in direct proportion to the number of dollars available.

You're seeking the wrong form of support—As a whole, foundations shy away from giving certain forms of support. For instance, they generally do not like to provide funds for:

General operating expenses. (If you have a general-operating expense need, then emphasize its special significance.)

Building and other construction projects. (Foundations usually prefer to support services and research activities.)

Noninnovative projects. (Many foundations enjoy the thrill of supporting fresh ideas; pilot projects and feasibility studies are especially popular.)

Maintenance of existing programs. (It is unlikely that a foundation will adopt you in midstream; even a foundation that has been supporting you from your earliest days may choose to discontinue its funding.)

Emergency funding. (Foundations are adverse to giving twelfth-hour funding.)

Of course, there are always exceptions to these rules, as is illustrated by the IRS Form 990-AR sample in Appendix E. (The Olin Foundation heavily supported construction grants.)

You lack a track record—Understandably foundations demand evidence of your capability. If you are a new organization, they want to know the past accomplishments of your staff, officers, and board members.

Other Factors Foundations Look For

Each foundation has its own methods for choosing grantees, and sometimes even two executives within the same foundation will use different criteria. The type of foundation you're approaching is another variable. (For insights, see Part II, "How Foundations Differ.")

Yet despite these differences among foundations, there are certain questions that most foundation executives ask themselves when evaluating a proposal. These questions include the points raised in the first half of Step 2 and those below. A few are similar to the ones you asked yourself in Step 1.

Does the project satisfy our grant-making policy in terms of field of interest? Type of grant? Size of grant? Length of grant period? Geographical restrictions?

How significant is the need? Who will benefit if the need is solved? Is the need documented?

Will the suggested solution work? Is the solution cost-effective? Is the timing right for solving the problem? Is the grant-seeker employing the best methods? Are the methods specific in detailing who will do what, why, when, where, and how?

Will the success of the project have a positive and far-reaching impact beyond itself? Will a project failure muddy the water for any future attempt by another organization to solve the problem?

Is the project a good investment for our foundation in terms of our available assets and other pending grant requests?

Is the organization qualified to undertake the project in terms of staff, leadership, and facilities? In terms of the personal character and integrity of the key people involved? Do the key personnel know their field and understand the full complexity and scope of the problem? Are the personnel enthusiastic about the project? Is the project a top priority for the organization? Does the organization have the right contacts to accomplish its objectives?

Does the project overlap or duplicate other programs—past, present, or planned? Is there a more qualified organization to handle the project?

Is the budget realistic? Is it sufficiently detailed?

Can the success of the project be measured and evaluated? By whom? When? How?

Can the project backfire on us? Do we risk a legal suit, trouble with government authorities, or unfavorable publicity? Is there a chance that we might be trapped into the position of having to renew our grant for many years in order to keep the grant-seeker afloat?

Are we the best possible source for the needed funds?

Will the project's financial needs be partially met by other funding sources, including different foundations, members of the organization's board, community donations, and government agencies?

Most of the above questions and issues are discussed in greater detail in the various steps that follow.

Conclusion

By now you should have a good idea of whether it would be worthwhile for you to launch a grant-seeking campaign. If the answer is no, then we've saved you from wasting any further time, including the time it would take you to read the rest of this book. If, on the other hand, the answer is yes, then the suggestions and insights you'll find on the remaining pages will—hopefully—serve you well.

STEP 3

Organize Your Resources

Now that you have determined that your chances of success are favorable, you can prudently justify the cost of building and organizing your needed grant-seeking resources.

You need not be overly concerned with setting lines of responsibility and authority if your organization is small.

On the other hand, if your organization is large, formalized procedures are essential. At the onset your organization should select a key staff member to become the full- or part-time coordinator of the grant-seeking endeavor. (Presumably, this person will be you or someone you appoint.) The grant coordinator should become the central clearinghouse on all relevant information and work closely with your organization's development officer, should that position independently exist.

Internal Communications

Creating and maintaining good internal communications are vital to the project's ultimate success. Therefore the first responsibilities of the new grant coordinator should be:

To discuss the project with the staff—perhaps even to brainstorm with them for new approaches and ideas.

To prepare a brief written summary of the grant project and to distribute it to all personnel concerned.

Reference Library

Although every professional grant-seeker has an idea of what the basic grant reference library should contain, virtually all would agree that the following resources are indispensable to the serious grant-seeker:

Foundation Directory and *Supplements.*

Foundation Grants Index (*Annual* and *Bimonthly* editions).

Individual files on key foundation prospects, containing collected data such as IRS Forms 990 and 990-ARs, annual reports, correspondence, and custom research reports prepared by either the grant-seeker or an outside professional service.

These tools, plus a host of other valuable information resources, are described in Part III.

Your "Competition"—A Data Source

Don't isolate yourself from your "competition": those organizations seeking funds from the same foundations you are courting. Meet with your counterparts over lunch or a drink and freely share information. You'll learn more about the foundations you're investigating, and you'll probably also learn of new funding sources you never previously considered. In the long run you and your competition will mutually benefit.

Start Building Contacts—Now

If your organization doesn't already have a circle of influential friends supporting it, then you should try doubly hard to gain this support now. Backing from these people can be very helpful when you make your initial contacts with foundations. For instance, one of your board members or volunteers might know a trustee on the board of a promising foundation prospect. While these match-ups never win a grant, they do make it easier to open doors and gain receptive audiences for your project.

Besides being well connected, board members can usually approach foundations more easily than organization staff members. And, as unpaid volunteers, they are in a better position to establish your organization's credibility in the eyes of the foundation.

If your current board has no influential contacts, then suggest to your leadership that the board be reorganized. If the uninfluential members have other qualities, then merely suggest an expansion of the existing board. In short, each board member should contribute something to the organization (money, contacts, influence, prestige, wisdom, expertise in your field) and, collectively, the board should be well balanced.

You and your fellow executives should begin to extend your circle of contacts. Become a joiner.

If possible, cultivate good relations with your representative in Congress. The fruits of your efforts will include introductions and easier access to government data and agencies. However, don't expect too much Congressional support unless your project involves public works, affects a large segment of the representative's constituency, and/or requires a large sum of money.

Although developing personal contacts is all-important in grant-seeking, never try to marshall too much "third-party" pressure, whether from board members or your Washington representative. Foundation executives almost always react negatively to outside pressure. And, of course, third-party endorsement can never take the place of a well-conceived, well-organized grant project.

STEP 4

Identify Your Prospects

The shotgun approach is one of the most inefficient ways to seek grants. We know of many instances in which grant-aspirants invested much postage and paper in sending mass-produced mailings to numerous foundations. One hopeful broadsided 10,000.

Needless to say, that technique proved costly as well as futile. The fund-seeker would have been better advised to use a rifle approach by:

Researching and compiling a preliminary list of the most promising foundations (perhaps twenty-five).

Researching each of the foundations in depth for the purpose of narrowing down the list to a chosen few (perhaps ten).

Approaching each of these chosen few on an individualized basis.

Looking for Grant Patterns

Your research task is to identify those foundations that have funded projects similar to yours in purpose, field of interest, size, or locale. For example, your chances of being funded by a particular foundation are slim if:

You're seeking funds to build a new dormitory, but the foundation has never funded construction projects.

Your field is the performing arts, but the foundation has a history of supporting medical research projects.

You need $100,000, but the foundation has never granted more than $5,000 to any single project.

You're located in San Francisco, but the foundation has funded projects only in Los Angeles.

The Foundation Center, through its various publications and library services, is by far the best source for researching grant patterns. Below are brief instructions for using three of its tools:

FOUNDATION GRANTS INDEX—This annual book and its bimonthly updates contain descriptions of recently reported grants of $5,000 or more. Use the *Index* to find the names of foundations funding projects similar to yours. To locate the appropriate grant listings, look in:

the "Recipient" index to find the names of funded organizations with projects similar to yours.

the "Key Words and Phrases" index for brief descriptions that relate to your project.

Or, because grants are listed by state, you can make a search for all the grants made in your locality. See Part Three for more detailed instructions on using the *Foundation Grants Index.*

COMPUTERIZED SEARCH—Another way to identify foundations funding projects similar to yours is to use the Foundation Center's computerized data banks. You can order a computer printout of those grants containing the key words and phrases you have selected. See Part III for a more detailed description.

FOUNDATION DIRECTORY—This book contains brief descriptions of some 2,500 large foundations. Since the *Directory* is arranged by states, you can make a foundation-by-foundation search for the key prospects in your locale. Look for grant policies and characteristics such as field of interest. See Part Three for a more thorough analysis of the *Directory*.

There are many other information sources, including books and professional consulting services, that you can use to help you identify grant patterns. These are also described in Part III.

STEP 5

Research Your Prospects in Depth

Now that you have assembled a preliminary list of promising foundations, your next step is to narrow the field to a chosen few through in-depth research. Your criteria should be:

GRANT PATTERNS—Including the purpose, size, and recipient. (You must research these factors in greater breadth and detail than you did in Step 4.)

DISTANCE—Becomes relevant whenever a meeting with a faraway foundation entails substantial travel expenses.

LEADERSHIP MATCH-UP—For example, does one of your directors know one of the trustees?

GENERAL ACCESSIBILITY—How easy will it be to open communications and arrange a meeting?

TYPE OF FOUNDATION—For insights see Part Two, "How Foundations Differ."

Foundation Fact Sheet

To collect and organize this data some type of standard form is helpful, if not essential. Whatever form you use, be sure to keep it simple. Over-complicated record-keeping systems are time-absorbing as well as incomprehensible to new staff members. We also suggest that you give your form ample white space. Tightly packed forms may save you paper and subsequent duplicating costs, but they are inflexible.

For your convenience a suggested "Foundation Fact Sheet," complete with sample entries, follows. Adapt this form to suit your specific needs.

FOUNDATION FACT SHEET

FOUNDATION: Mythical Foundation
GRANT SOUGHT: $100,000 to computerize our medical research
 library
DATE OF REPORT: March 16, 1975
PREPARED BY: Dr. R.D. Simpson
. . . .
ADDRESS AND TELEPHONE NUMBER:
 Mythical Foundation
 502 N. Dearborn Street
 Chicago, Ill. 60610
 (312) 618-8830

PREVIOUS CONTACT WITH FOUNDATION:
 None

TYPE OF FOUNDATION:
 Family

SOURCE OF FUNDS:
 Bequest by the late M. M. Mythical, founder of the Mythical Drug
 Store chain

ASSETS (including date, and whether market or ledger value):
$5,040,000 market value (as of January 16, 1975)

TOTAL ANNUAL GRANTS, NUMBER, AND RANGE (and year of
record):

1973 $\begin{cases} \text{total: } \$332,000 \\ \text{number: } 18 \\ \text{range: } \$2,500 \text{ to } \$105,000 \end{cases}$

GRANT POLICIES AND PATTERNS. DESCRIPTIONS OF RELEVANT
GRANTS:
Strong interest in higher education.

Virtually all funds have gone to institutions within a 50-mile
radius of Chicago.

Has funded three library-related projects during the last two
years of record:

$42,000 to Fisher University
in matching funds for
construction of $1,200,000
library wing (1973)

$60,000 to Hamlyn College
to underwrite the cost of a
summer seminar for small-
college librarians (1973)

$27,500 to Woodbury Public
Library for purchase of books
for its American Indian
Collection (1972)

According to well-informed sources, Woodbury Public Library is
currently proposing a $58,000 grant to expand its American
Indian Collection.

OFFICERS AND TRUSTEES (attach "bio sheets"):
    John Doe—President and Trustee
    Warren Todd—Secretary
    Jane Mythical—Trustee
    Roberta Mythical—Trustee
    Peter Smith—Trustee
    Richard Ward—Trustee
    George Weinstein—Trustee

APPLICATION DEADLINE(S):
    February 1 and September 1, every year

DATE(S) WHEN BOARD OF TRUSTEES MEET:
    Third Tuesday in March and October, every year

BASIC STRATEGY (preliminary):
    This is very much a "local" foundation. As a result we should
    try hard to find match-ups between our trustees, administrators,
    faculty and alumni, and the foundation's trustees and officers.

    I believe we should emphasize to the foundation that our project
    is pilot in nature. If our project can be implemented successfully,
    it will serve as a "guiding light" for other medical schools across
    the country.

    Because of the size of the grant President Stanley Columbo
    should sign the letter of inquiry and be the chief spokesman at
    the meeting with the foundation if one can be arranged.

Circulating the Foundation Fact Sheets

Once having compiled the "Foundation Fact Sheets," you
are ready to duplicate them for circulation to your trustees,
key administrators, and influential friends. Your purpose is
twofold:

To pick their brains for ideas.

To discover if they know (or know someone who knows) any of the foundation's trustees or officers.

Matching up your people with those of the foundation is extremely important. This is especially true if the foundation is small or medium-sized because they tend to be more receptive to personal contacts than the larger, more formally run foundations.

To jog the memory of your people, attach to the Foundation Fact Sheets individual "bio sheets" on the foundation trustees and officers, giving social and business ties. The prime source for this kind of information is usually *Who's Who in America,* or one of its regional or industrial editions. To illustrate, here is a sample listing:

ROCKEFELLER, NELSON ALDRICH, former gov. of N.Y.; b. Bar Harbor, Me., July 8, 1908; s. John Davison, Jr., and Abby Greene (Aldrich) R.; prep. edn. Lincoln Sch. of Tchrs. Coll., N.Y.C., 1917-26; A.B., Dartmouth, 1930; m. Mary Todhunter Clark, June 23, 1930 (div. 1962); children—Rodman, Ann (Mrs. Ann R. Coste) and Steven (twins), Michael (dec.), Mary (Mrs. Mary R. Strawbridge); m. 2d, Margaretta Fitler Murphy, May, 1963; children—Nelson A., Mark F. Dir. Rockefeller Center, Inc., 1931-58, pres., 1938-45, 1948-51, chmn., 1945-53, 1956-58; coordinator of Inter-Am. Affairs, 1940-44; asst. sec. of state, 1944-45; chmn. Devel. Adv. Bd. (point 4 program), 1950-51; under sec. health, edn. and welfare 1953-54; spl. asst. to Pres., 1954-55; gov. of N.Y., 1958-73; chmn. Commn. on Critical Choices for Am., 1973—; chmn. Commn. Water Quality, 1972—. Chmn. Human Resources Com. Gov.'s Conf.; mem. Pres. Adv. Commn. Intergovtl. Relations, 1965-69. Treas. Mus. Modern Art, 1935-39, trustee, 1932—, pres. 1939-41, 1946-53, chmn., 1957-58; founder, trustee, pres. Mus. Primitive Art; trustee Rockefeller Bros. Fund, Inc.; chmn. Pres.' adv. com. govt. orgn., 1953-58. Awarded Order of Merit of Chile, by Pres. Rios, 1945; Nat. Order So. Cross (Brazil), 1946; Order of the Aztec Eagle (Mexico), 1949; Gold medal award Nat. Inst. Social Scis., 1967; Conservation and Water Mgmt. award Gt. Lakes Commn., 1970. others. Mem. Psi Upsilon, Phi Beta Kappa. Baptist. Clubs: Century Assn., Dartmouth (N.Y.C.); Cosmos (Washington). Author:

The Future of Federalism, 1962; Unity, Freedom
and Peace, 1968; Our Environment Can Be
Saved, 1970. Home: Pocantico Hills North Tarry-
town NY 10591 Office: State Capitol Albany
NY 12202

Copyright ©, 1974, by Marquis Who's Who, Incorporated

For details on *Who's Who in America,* your local *Social
Register* and other biographically rich sources, see Part III.

Assign Priorities

With your researched data in hand, including the "who
knows who" information, you are in position to set priorities
as to which foundations to approach first. Use the criteria
outlined in the early part of this chapter. As to weighting,
that's a decision that must be based on the factors affecting
your individual situation.

There are a number of rating codes used by professional
grant-seekers. Some rate by stars (* to ****), a few use
percentages (0 percent to 100 percent) while others use the
age-old classroom system (A, B, C, D and F). It doesn't
really matter which coding method you use, providing you
feel comfortable with it and all the people working with
you understand and accept it.

Updating Your Records

Your records must be continually revised and reevaluated
if you are to be successful over the long term. New data
flows in steadily from established sources, such as from the
newly revised editions of the standard reference books. In
addition, there is a stream of new information too fresh to
have been included in these standard reference books. Keep

an alert eye for this kind of information in newspapers and
magazines. For example, a recent news article told of plans
to establish the Geraldine Rockefeller Dodge Foundation
with $85 million in assets (that would qualify it as one of
America's 100 largest foundations) for "charitable, scientific, literary, artistic and educational purposes, and for the
prevention of cruelty to animals." The resourceful grant-
seeker will get a headstart on those who wait until this information is published in the directories.

STEP 6

Make Your Initial Contact

Equipped with information on your key prospects, you are well armed to make your first contact with each foundation.

Opening up a dialogue with a foundation is not always easy—and sometimes it is impossible. But once two-way communication is established, you can determine whether further dealings with the foundation are a good investment on your part. If the answer is no, you can direct your time and resources to more productive areas.

Unless the foundation headquarters are distantly located, your primary purpose in making the first contact should be to arrange an exploratory meeting between appropriate representatives from your organization and the foundation. A face-to-face meeting is highly desirable because:

The Human Element—Foundation executives are professional, yet still human like the rest of us. They will tend to take a greater interest once person-to-person contact has been made because you will no longer be an abstraction on a piece of paper. A meeting also allows the foundation official to assess character, a quality that is difficult to judge from a written proposal.

Fact Finding—You'll receive the latest official foundation guidelines firsthand. You'll also gain information sometimes not published or given in correspondence (for instance: "preferred format" and "number of copies desired"). And you may even learn of forthcoming policy changes.

Question Asking—It is usually easier and more productive to ask questions in a meeting than by letter, especially if the questions are touchy. Suggested questions are given in "Step 7—Meet with the Foundation."

Feedback—You'll gain insights and sometimes advice on writing your proposal, including what turns that particular foundation on and off. In some cases, the feedback will be 100 percent negative: "We're not interested." That in itself is valuable information because you won't be wasting any further time and resources on a misdirected hunt.

Special Assistance—Some foundation officers may freely give you general advice on how to make your proposal more appealing to other foundations. They might even give you the names of (and sometimes introductions to) promising funding sources.

The initial contact can be formally made through a letter, by telephone, or via a cold office call; or perhaps informally made if someone associated with your organization personally knows one of the foundation officers or trustees. Make your request several weeks before the date of your desired meeting.

Arranging the Meeting—by Telephone

Most professional grant-seekers, though not all, believe you should first attempt to set up a meeting by telephone, not through a letter. After all, they argue, the biggest tragedy that can befall you is that the foundation will tell you to write your request—and you might in the process gain the specific information as to whom, what, when, where, and how to write.

Telephoning has other advantages. It can produce a quick answer as to whether and when the meeting is to take place. If you speak with the right person, you can also gain immediate insight into the foundation's probable degree of interest without waiting for a written reply.

When and if you reach an executive, be prepared. You should have your opening line well rehearsed. State your purpose in clear and simple terms, suggest that the meeting be brief (15 to 30 minutes), and don't hesitate to mention the name of a prominent person associated with your organization.

Have all essential data at your fingertips. Bring the foundation and the executive into the picture by tailoring your approach to them. Put yourself in their shoes. Be careful not to say anything that might be misunderstood or controversial. These matters are suitably broached in the meeting.

Be enthusiastic and persuasive, but don't oversell. Avoid revealing too much of your program or else the foundation executive may see little reason to schedule a meeting. Finally, keep detailed records of your conversation for future use.

If the executive refuses to schedule an appointment, then ask if a letter of inquiry would be welcomed. If the executive is merely hesitant about scheduling the meeting, then suggest a tentative appointment for a specific date. As most salespersons know, tentative appointments have a way of becoming firm ones. Once your name is on the calendar, it takes a conscious decision by the executive to remove it.

The two chief drawbacks to telephoning are:

You can be asked those embarrassing, unexpected, probing
questions. Remember, a foundation executive is usually a
skilled master of this art.

Some people do not have pleasing telephone voices, are not
good salespersons and/or are not gifted in thinking quickly on
their feet. The telephone is seldom a viable medium for anyone fitting one or more of these descriptions.

If you do decide to call, be sure you've done your homework on the foundation, on the person you're calling, and
on your own organization and its field. This knowledge will
not only make you more confident and compelling, it will
also minimize futile telephone calls.

Your first hurdle in securing an appointment is getting
by the secretary, who can range in the Hollywood stereotype
from the friendly person who can't do too much for you to
the impregnable screen through which no unsolicited call
ever passes. If you encounter the latter, don't fight the situation—it could backfire on you later. Instead, try to set up
the appointment through the secretary. Should that line of
attack also fail, at least try to gain as much information as
you can about application procedures.

Once being granted the appointment, give a quick but
polite thank you and good-by. Many a long-winded caller
has talked the appointment off the calendar.

Immediately follow up your successful call with a con-
firming letter. It gives you a chance to put in writing the
salient points covered in your telephone call. The letter
serves two other purposes as well: it reinforces you and
your organization's existence in the executive's mind, and

it insures against the possibility that he or his secretary neglected to record the appointment on his calendar.

Arranging the Meeting—by Letter

. As with the telephone call, the purpose of the letter of inquiry is to win an interview—or, at least, to gain an early indication of the foundation's degree of interest in your project.

Keep the letter of inquiry brief (seldom more than one typewritten page; shorter if possible). Come straight to the point: you want a meeting. Tailor the letter to the foundation and stress its opportunity, not your need. Be positive and convincing, but low-keyed (for example: "We would like you to consider . . .").

Unless you have information to the contrary, address the letter to the president of a small foundation and to the executive secretary or director of a large one. Rarely should your formal letter of inquiry be sent to a trustee.

Your letter should usually be signed by your president or a distinguished board member. On occasion, however, there may be a special reason why it should be signed by the grant-coordinator or development officer.

While the letter's content and topical sequence may vary, you might find the following approach useful:

1. State your purpose (to secure an interview, perhaps 20 to 30 minutes in length).
2. Briefly describe your project, including its objective, significance, and uniqueness.
3. State the cost, duration of the project, and the type of funding you seek (full grant, matching grant, etc.).

4. Tell why you believe the project would interest the foundation.
5. Provide relevant background information on your organization—perhaps with an attached brochure or fact sheet. Highlight your salient points, including achievements, previous grants, staff qualifications, and well-known people associated with your organization. Give an honest appraisal of your organization and the way in which it fits into its field.
6. Volunteer to furnish additional information if requested.
7. Restate your request for a meeting to discuss the project in greater depth.

Keep in mind that your letter of inquiry will be read by human beings, not the foundation entity. As you write, imagine that you are talking face to face with the intended reader. Also try to understand the reader's needs. For instance, the foundation executive is as susceptible to the "security factor" as most of us. In self-defense the evaluator will be searching for reasons why your project could fail or backfire.

Don't wait for a reply too eagerly. Your letter may not be answered even with a mimeographed "thank you, but no thank you" card. Many foundations, especially the smaller ones, do not welcome unsolicited inquiries.

Arranging the Meeting—via a Cold Office Call

Calling upon an officer without an appointment has proven successful for some grant-seekers, but their number is small. Of the several techniques for approaching foundations this is the least effective, and it often rankles a foundation executive. Your uninvited "intrusion" may also lead the executive to the conclusion that your grant-seeking endeavor lacks adequate preparation.

Arranging the Meeting—by Informal Contact

Perhaps someone associated with your organization knows one of the key foundation officers or trustees. In that case, ask the person to make an informal overture by means of a personal letter, telephone call or visit—perhaps during a friendly round of golf.

Who Should Attend the Meeting

There is no hard-and-fast rule as to who or how many people should attend the meeting. Possibilities include the grant-coordinator, development officer, president, department heads, noted faculty members, distinguished alumni, trustees, and influential friends of your organization who happen to know the foundation official.

Determining factors include:

Grant Size—The bigger the grant, the bigger the guns you want to bring along.

Organization Size—The larger your organization, the less likely it is that your president will have the time to attend the meeting.

Position of Foundation Official—In most cases your representative should be on the same level as the foundation official.

Type of Foundation—In the case of a small family foundation you will probably meet with an outside professional (attorney, bank trust officer, etc.) who serves as a part-time administrator. With larger foundations, you will probably meet with a full-time administrator (who might be a specialist in your particular field of interest).

Technical Complexity—You might consider having experts attend the meeting if your project is highly technical.

Subsequent Meetings—If there is to be more than one meeting, you might consider saving the time of your higher-ups by having a lower-echelon staff member do the initial groundwork at the first meeting. But make sure that this person is a capable spokesperson for your organization; otherwise the foundation official may cancel or not schedule further meetings.

Individual Qualities—Whoever attends (especially your spokesperson) should be well informed about your project and the foundation, should be a good salesperson, and should be capable of generating a positive rapport with the foundation official.

In most instances the meeting is kept small and the grant-coordinator (or development officer) attends, but plays a supporting role. There are some cases where only two people are present—the foundation official and your representative.

Other Special Tips and Insights

Appointment-Making Ease—Generally speaking it is easier to obtain an appointment with a large, professionally staffed foundation. But a small foundation offers you a better chance to use well-placed contacts if you have them.

How Many Foundations Should You Contact?—The answer: each of your chosen few—and, later on, selected foundations lower down on your key prospect list. Above all, don't send multi-copies if you are using the letter approach. Personalize and individually type each communication.

Proper Channels—End-running a foundation official by dealing outside the proper channels usually spells disaster, especially if a large foundation is involved. Without question, there are valid reasons to communicate with a trustee —perhaps to test the waters, or to establish the initial dialogue with the foundation, or because you know the trustee personally. But when you do contact a trustee, inform the foundation officer of this fact. Keep this executive apprised of all future dealings that might infringe upon his administrative authority and responsibility.

Trustee Support—With smaller foundations, some experienced grant-seekers have found it useful to enlist a trustee to act as their advocate at the board meeting. If that tactic violates board rules (and it usually does), then try to persuade a trustee to assume the role of an impartial overseer of your proposal. Having a "friend in the court" doesn't usually sway the board's vote, but it helps prevent your proposal from being misunderstood or given a cursory review.

Backup Material—Furnishing the foundation with quality brochures and other backup material is to your advantage. However, if these supporting documents look too expensive, they may boomerang. The foundation executives and board members may think your organization is wasting money on nonessentials.

STEP 7

Meet With the Foundation

Let's assume you've been successful in your quest to set up an exploratory meeting with the foundation. (If not, see the "If No Meeting" section at the end of this chapter.) Your immediate goal is to prepare yourself as fully as possible because:

You will probably not have another opportunity to gain firsthand feedback and to sell your project in person. More often than not this meeting will be your only face-to-face encounter with the foundation official before you submit your proposal—if you're invited to do so at all.

Even if you do have subsequent meetings, first impressions tend to be lasting. Put your best foot forward.

While the final decision rests with the board of trustees, foundation executives can influence the board's decision. They wield substantial power through their recommendations, often by keeping the proposal from appearing on the board's agenda in the first place. With so many proposals to screen, foundation executives usually find it easier to look for reasons why a proposal should not be reviewed by the board than to find reasons why it should be.

Preparing for the Meeting

Foundation executives will surely ask you hard-nosed, probing questions during the interview. That's their job. The best way to prepare for the proposal-dissecting encounter is to role-play with your associates. Hazy thinking and missing facts will quickly be exposed. At the same time, the rehearsals will help make you psychologically confident.

Just before the meeting, refresh your memory with all significant facts and details, and review your plan of action.

If you're not the head of your delegation at the meeting, then be sure you give the designated speaker all pertinent information, including a brief rundown on your strategy and any previous dealings with the foundation. You might also provide biographical information that will allow your representative to break the ice at the meeting. For example, your representative could say, "I understand that you are a trustee at the First National Bank. Perhaps you know my cousin, one of the bank's vice presidents."

Do's and Dont's at the Meeting

You're now sitting down at the meeting, ready for action. Keep in mind these do's and don'ts:

Do keep the meeting short (15 to 30 minutes) and use this time well.

Do create a friendly, open atmosphere. Be confident and enthusiastic, but professional.

Do be brief and to the point. Never use trade jargon unless you're certain the foundation executive is well versed in it and appreciates its use.

Do be honest and accurate. Never stretch the truth. Foundation
executives are experienced hyperbole-sleuths.

Don't knock your "competition."

Don't oversell yourself. This approach may raise doubts in a
foundation executive's mind.

Do ask questions. (See the "Questions to Ask" section which
immediately follows.)

Do listen carefully.

Don't press for a decision.

Do think of the long term. If the foundation executive is against
or even unfairly critical of your project, try to leave on a
positive note, keeping the door open for future proposals.

Don't dally. Leave before the pace of the meeting slackens.

Questions to Ask

Take full advantage of the meeting by asking pertinent
questions. Here are a few you might pose to the foundation
official, depending on the circumstances:

What specific suggestions do you have for the proposal's content? Format? Length? Style?

When is the application deadline? If we submit our proposal
early, will it be assigned a better position on the board's
agenda?

When does the Board of Trustees meet?

How many copies of the proposal would you prefer? If we give
you extra copies early, will you distribute them in advance to
the board members?

What do your board members particularly look for? What dis-
pleases them?

May we submit more than one specific proposal, allowing your
board to choose among them?

Would you make constructive suggestions on our proposal if we
sent you a draft?

Would you be willing to visit our facilities?

Would you give us general advice on our project that would improve our chances with other foundations? Could you suggest other funding sources and, possibly, introduce us to them?

Additional Meetings

Sometimes subsequent meetings are arranged to clear up vague or unsettled questions and issues. These get-togethers vary in character from the initial meeting and usually they are attended by higher-echelon personnel.

A second meeting gives you the chance to reemphasize the reasons why your project is an opportunity for the foundation. Another plus: the foundation executive might review and make suggestions for improving your proposal draft.

Your facilities are an ideal place to hold the second meeting. Take the initiative and suggest that possibility to the foundation. An on-sight inspection tour will personalize your organization and staff in the minds of the visiting officials.

If No Meeting

In most instances your preliminary letter of inquiry (or telephone call) will not produce an appointment from the foundation because:

The foundation has read your letter and is not interested.
The foundation hasn't read your letter. (It was thrown in the wastepaper basket.)
The foundation does not grant interviews as a matter of policy. (All dealings are conducted through the mail.)

Quite often you have no way of knowing which of these reasons was the culprit because your letter was never answered at all. In such a case there is nothing to do but perhaps try again at a later date, hoping that policy, personnel, or happenstance change. However, you may wish to submit a more-detailed letter of inquiry, or perhaps the formal proposal itself if—and only if—you believe special circumstances warrant it.

If you do receive a letter from the foundation, you could simply be informed that the foundation doesn't schedule (or, in your case, wish to schedule) meetings. Unless you believe the foundation's answer was a polite turndown, revise your letter of inquiry to ask for an invitation to submit your proposal.

Still another possibility is the straightforward "We're not interested" reply. Don't waste any more time. Go on to greener pastures.

The response could also say that the foundation doesn't schedule meetings, but invites you to submit a formal proposal. Do so with gusto. Chances are you have a hot prospect.

Sometimes the initial letter of inquiry is written not to ask for a meeting, but rather to test the waters or to request permission to submit the formal proposal. This latter tactic is frequently used if the foundation is far away or is known to have a no-meeting policy. To write this type of letter, simply substitute your "proposal submission request" for the "meeting request" in the letter of inquiry outlined previously on page 43. The rest of the letter's content and its form will remain the same.

STEP 8

Write Your Formal Proposal

Your formal proposal is all-important. This paper document is likely to be your only representative at the foundation's board meeting, and a small detail you include (or neglect to include) could spell the difference between receiving a check or a rejection letter.

The time has come to sit down and write your proposal. Relax; it's not that difficult. If you've done the preliminary work described in the preceding steps and if you follow the suggestions outlined in this chapter, you will find proposal-writing less burdensome than you imagined.

Your proposal is but one of three parts of the total package you send to the foundation. The other two parts—the cover letter and the addendum—are described at the end of this chapter. Until then, we'll be focusing attention on the proposal, the primary part of your presentation.

Proposal Format

Unfortunately for grant-seekers, the foundation field does not have a standard format for the proposal. In fact, practically no foundation publishes, let alone suggests, preferred formats.

What then do you do? We suggest you adopt the format frequently used by management personnel in all disciplines, including those of the grant-seeking field. Whatever the executive is requesting, be it a new plant in Idaho or approval of a marketing plan, the proposal should flow logically from:

THE NEED

↓

THE OBJECTIVE

↓

THE METHODS

↓

THE BUDGET

The "objective" should be a direct outgrowth of the "need." Likewise, the "methods" should be a function of the "objective," while the "budget" should be determined by the "methods."

In addition, the proposal should contain: a brief introduction and summary for the busy reader; the qualifications of the people undertaking the project; a program to measure and evaluate the results; the future of the project (if there is to be one).

If you already have your own tried and proven format, then use it. Otherwise, use the eight-section format we've outlined below. (Adjust it to special circumstances, should they exist.) Each section is described separately in the pages that follow:

    I. Introduction and Summary

    II. The Need

    III. The Objective

    IV. The Methods

    V. Organization Qualifications

    VI. The Evaluation

    VII. The Budget

    VIII. The Program's Future

Foundation proposals vary in length from 1 to 50 pages. However, most foundation executives prefer short proposals —ideally not more than 4 single-spaced or 8 double-spaced typewritten pages, excluding the title page. Reason: any project taking more space than this to describe is probably not carefully thought out.

Sometimes a program can be presented effectively in only 1 or 2 pages. In that case, consider putting the proposal in a letter rather than in a more formal format.

Your final draft should be typed by a skilled secretary.

A document laden with erasure and white-out marks can detract from your message.

Unless you happen to be writing a proposal for an ecology project, let your pages breathe with white space. Use wide margins and double spacing.

Another way to make your pages easy to read is to break up long copy by using indentations and subheadings. Underlining can be effective in emphasizing key points if employed judiciously.

The original copy should be sent to the foundation. Extra copies (such as those requested for foundation trustees) may be photocopied rather than typed.

People do sometimes judge a proposal by its physical appearance; consequently, packaging your proposal is important. Do use quality materials, but not too expensive lest the foundation think you squander money. Shun gimmicks. Avoid anything that might smack of gaudiness. Finally, use a protective envelope to prevent damage in transit.

Writing Tips

Many a good idea has remained fundless because its creator didn't know the ins and outs of writing a good proposal. Though there is no set formula for success, we hope the following tips prove useful:

The first rule: if you don't have writing talent and experience, find someone who does—even if you have to pay for this service.

The second rule: get started. As with most tasks, once you take the first few steps, your momentum builds. Write your first draft today. Don't be concerned about grammar or spelling. You can correct such errors in later drafts.

Come to the point—early. Rightfully assume that the foundation executive doesn't have enough time to read thoroughly all the proposals arriving in the mail. Give all the essentials in the opening paragraphs.

Tell why your project is significant and why it will have impact beyond the project itself. For example, your success could pave the way for your counterparts in other cities.

Point out clearly and early the link between your project and the foundation's field of interest. In other words, describe how your project would fulfill the foundation's grant-making goals.

Don't be afraid to state up front how much the project will cost. This is one of the first questions a foundation executive wants answered. If the figure seems too high or too low for the foundation, then you are probably approaching the wrong funding source in the first place.

If you are seeking only a one-time grant, make sure you point out this fact to the foundation. Your action will help relieve the foundation's concern that it may be forced to adopt you financially in the years to come.

If you have other funding sources, then state so. Foundations feel more secure when they know that others are also supporting a project they are considering.

Incorporate only the most significant supportive data in the body of the proposal. Put the rest in your addendum.

Don't leave anything for the reader to guess or assume. If you didn't include something in your proposal or addendum, then the foundation executive will probably conclude that it wasn't part of your program, or—even worse—that you overlooked it through ignorance.

Be sure to incorporate into your final proposal the feedback you've received during your meetings with the foundation.

Anticipate your reader's faultfinding questions. For example, omit statements that might lead the foundation executive to think your project is too ambitious, too premature or vague, or that the solution is more complex than you realize.

Write to a human being, not to the abstract foundation entity.

Imagine your reader sitting across the desk from you and reacting to your words and the way you express yourself.

Take into account the "security factor" of the foundation executive. Like most of us, foundation officials and trustees are cautious about making mistakes that could jeopardize their jobs or professional standing. Therefore, allaying their personal fears is a vital ingredient in a successful proposal.

Focus on the human element, not on theoretical ideas and buildings. Describe how people will benefit from your programs and facilities.

Use exciting language. For example, use the active voice ("We will solve the problem") rather than the passive voice ("The problem will be solved by us"). Also use image-provoking adjectives ("the hungry child") if they describe conditions accurately.

Be brief and concise in your writing. At the same time use a warm narrative style. Cold, impersonal writing seldom touches the reader's heart.

Use simple words. Two-dollar words slow down the reader. The same is true for awkward or complex sentence structure.

Use footnotes for explanations that might slow down the smooth flow of the proposal. But don't overuse them, or they'll become cumbersome in themselves.

Try to avoid professional jargon (even if you know the principal reader is an expert in your field). If a technical or unfamiliar word must be used, define it in layman's terms. Someone on the board of trustees might not understand trade vocabulary.

Be clear, and make sure you realize the innuendos of all the words and phrases you use.

Be specific. Use concrete examples and facts to support your case. Sweeping generalizations and hazy thinking cause foundation executives to wince.

Build credibility. Be straightforward and frank about both your strengths and limitations. But when you discuss your shortcomings, use a positive, nonapologetic tone.

Be objective. Refrain from using superlatives or other forms of rhetoric. Overselling and glamorizing your project or organization lowers rather than raises your image in the eyes of the foundation executive.

Project optimism and confidence without seeming unrealistic or boastful. Be enthusiastic, but don't get carried away, or the foundation executive might think that your feet aren't on the ground.

Write, edit, and rewrite your proposal—again and again. Read your drafts into a tape recorder. Lack of flow and smoothness will become immediately apparent.

Enlist others to read and criticize your proposal. These people should include your staff members and experts, especially if the field is technical. Other readers should be people who are unfamiliar with your project, but who are generally acquainted with your field. When selecting the third-party readers, make sure they are willing and able to give constructive criticism.

Steer clear of committee writing. Obtain criticism and ideas from others, but in the end let one person "mastermind" the final draft. A cohesive writing style will result.

Finally, remember your application becomes a legal contract, once approved. Be sure you can deliver everything you promise.

Writing the Title Page

The following format, with possible minor adjustments, should prove effective for you:

a proposal for a
$100,000 GRANT

to establish
A SUMMER CAMP FOR NEEDY CHILDREN

submitted to
THE XYZ FOUNDATION

on
October 31, 1975

by
Your name
Your title
YOUR ORGANIZATION
Your address
Your telephone number

Don't be afraid to state on the title page how much money you are requesting. It's amazing how many grant-seekers bury this vital statistic in the body of their proposal, almost as if they were embarrassed by having to ask for money. Foundations are in business to give money away, and one of their very first questions is, "How much money is involved?" Tell them.

The title should be a one-sentence description of your project. If well-written, the reader should be able to grasp instantly what your project is trying to accomplish.

Whose name appears on the title sheet? The answer depends on your organization's operating procedures, but generally it's your project director, department chairman, executive director, president, or chairman of the board. In any case, this will be the person receiving the grant approval or rejection letter in the mail and the person who will be available for direct inquiries from the foundation, should they occur.

Writing the "Introduction and Summary" Section

This is the first section of your formal proposal, but don't try to write it first. Wait until you've finished drafting your "Need" through "Program's Future" sections. Then you'll be in a better position to summarize the essentials of your project.

From your "Introduction and Summary" section, the reader should be able to decide whether or not the project falls within the foundation's field of interest. If the answer is no, further reading would be unnecessary. If the answer is yes, the reader would be able to tackle the various sections of the proposal with greater perspective.

Keep the "Introduction" compact and to the point. The opening sentence or two should clearly and simply state your request. To illustrate:

"This is a request to the XYZ Foundation from ABC Organization for a two-year grant of $100,000 to create a neighborhood center for senior citizens."

Next, establish the need for your project and its significance, and tell whom it will benefit. Define your target population as specifically as possible by giving the geographic
scope and socio-economic status of the beneficiaries. If critical and relevant, provide background information on the
need.

Once you've described the need, relate it to the foundation's grant-making philosophy. Explain why your project
is an opportunity for the foundation to fulfill its goals, and
show the impact the grant will produce.

Your remaining task in the "Introduction and Summary"
section is perhaps the most important one: you must establish your credentials. Depending upon the particular circumstances, you should summarize:

Who you are by describing your organizational goals, key personnel (especially the program director), board members and
how all your contacts and expertise qualify you to solve the
need.

Your uniqueness in the field, and why you are the best available
organization to undertake this particular project.

Your history, including: date of establishment, success stories,
past funding sources, and previous contact with the foundation, if any.

How much community support you have, including the amount
and type of local resources already pledged for the project.

Any pertinent data, including an IRS Letter of Tax Exemption.

As you can see, you have much more to say in the "Introduction and Summary" section than you have space for, so
be selective. Save the non-highlights for the appropriate
sections that follow and for your addendum. To illustrate, if
you have a "highly qualified project director," simply state
so. The reader, if interested, will be able to find more specific

information in your "Qualifications" section, and perhaps still more detail in your addendum. That's where this type of data belongs.

Writing the "Need" Section

Many grant-seekers have been turned down by foundations because they tried to tackle more than they could possibly handle. You must narrow down your definition of need to that aspect of the problem which your organization can realistically solve, in terms of both time and resources.

For instance, it would be impractical for a medical-research team to attempt to find the "ultimate" cure for cancer. Its talent and the foundation's money would be more productively directed to investigating one particular facet of that disease.

Another error commonly committed by grant-seekers is not highlighting their project's significance by telling:

Who will benefit (including the number of beneficiaries, their geographical scope, and socio-economic status).
Who else in the community (besides the intended beneficiaries) is vitally concerned with the problem.

As we have emphasized before, clearly link the problem to the foundation's field of interest, and stress the foundation's opportunity, not your need.

Don't assume that the foundation will accept your unqualified assessment of need. Back your statements with supporting evidence. Use persuasive facts, expert opinions, the names of authorities and community leaders who can be contacted, and any other convincing documentation you can muster.

You must also establish that the problem isn't being solved, or will not be solved, by someone else. And you must prove to the foundation that you don't have adequate alternative funding sources (internal or external) for your project. One way to substantiate your claims is to provide verification letters from appropriate authorities.

Writing the "Objective" Section

All too many proposal writers confuse objectives with methods—two entirely different terms. An "objective" is what you want to achieve, while the "methods" are the manner in which you go about accomplishing your objectives. Another way to clarify the difference is to remember that "methods" are the means, while an "objective" is the end. To illustrate, one proposal writer mistakenly stated:

> "Our objective is to buy a mobile X-ray unit."

That's not the objective—it's the method. The proposal writer should have stated:

> "Our objective is to decrease the incidence of respiratory disease within our community."

Whatever your objective, it must be attainable, practical, and measurable. For it to be attainable, you must have the needed time and resources, including in-house expertise and community cooperation.

To be practical your project must produce results worthy of the investment you are asking a foundation to make. For example, an emergency helicopter ambulance service for Pikes Peak in Colorado would certainly benefit a few stranded mountain climbers, but wouldn't the cost of a helicopter and crew be better allocated towards a less "lofty" project benefiting more people?

To be measurable, the results must be capable of being objectively evaluated. For instance, in the case of the mobile X-ray unit, you could plan to compare the incidence of TB among your target population before and after your mobile unit was put into operation.

Word your objective in clear, concise language, being as specific and concrete as possible. If you have more than one objective, make your most important goal stand out by stating it first.

Writing the "Methods" Section

Your methods should be the ones that can most effectively accomplish your objective. Your "Methods" section should leave the foundation executive with a secure feeling that you know best how to go about achieving your objective. To create this security you must establish that:

You know what others in your field are doing and planning to do. For example, you have learned that a certain type of mobile van has proven to be the most cost-effective in other communities and is therefore probably the best choice for your project.

You are aware of all the options, and you know what methods work or don't work. To illustrate: in the case of the mobile X-ray unit, you know that setting up an information center to persuade the target population to go to the hospital for the needed X rays has been unsuccessful in your particular community.

You recognize the potential pitfalls and know how to protect yourself against them. For instance, you know that the temporary illness of the X-ray technician would immobilize the X-ray unit. Therefore you will arrange to have semi-retired technicians on call.

If possible, describe your methods in a step-by-step time-table format, either graphically or verbally. Most foundation executives welcome this approach because it helps them to understand priorities and chronological development. Be sure your timetable includes all the important milestones of your project.

Writing the "Qualifications" Section

This section helps assure the reader that your organization is qualified to undertake the project, and that no one else is better equipped to do so. In brief, you're building confidence and credibility. To convey these qualities most effectively try to include the following:

Your IRS Letter of Tax Exemption.

Your longevity and past successes. (If you're a new organization without a track record, emphasize the past accomplishments of your staff and board members.)

A brief description of the positions and responsibilities of key staff members. (If the relationships are many and complex, perhaps you can use an organizational chart.)

Biographical sketches of your key staff members. (Include résumés or vitae in the addendum when appropriate.)

Assurance that additional qualified personnel can be easily hired in case of staff turnover or expansion.

Description of your non-personnel resources: facilities, library collections, equipment, cooperative relationships, and programs with other organizations, to name a few.

Names, addresses, and telephone numbers of people who can be contacted to verify that your staff is competent and that your organization is the best one to undertake the project. But use references only if you have their permission.

Writing the "Evaluation" Section

Your evaluation system will serve three important purposes:

It will measure the degree of success of your completed project.
It will monitor the progress of your project (enabling you to readjust your methods and objectives in midstream if necessary).
It will help you determine whether your objective is measurable. (If it is not measurable, you will probably have a difficult time obtaining the grant.)

Too many proposal writers sidestep the responsibility of including an evaluation program by stating, "Our evaluation system will be established at the end of the project." This is copping out, and foundation executives know it.

You might consider having a third party design and execute your evaluation plan. If possible, find a distinguished person or institution to act as your evaluator. This will lend credibility to your project. Don't forget to include in your budget the cost of the evaluation program, whether paid for or donated.

Give the reader all pertinent data. Include a brief description of how the evaluation system works, the names and qualifications of the evaluator, and when and how the results will be reported.

When designing the system, avoid subjective criteria. For example, plans to solicit opinions on whether the project was successful are not enough, no matter how distinguished the opinion-givers. You need objective criteria such as "We will measure the change in library attendance before and after the library awareness-building project begins."

Put your evaluation system into operation at the beginning—or just before the beginning—of your project. Otherwise you won't be able to measure the change it can bring about. To illustrate: in the case of the library awareness-building campaign, you need to know the number and character of library users before you put your program into gear.

Writing the "Budget" Section

Your budget translates your methods into dollars. Although it's an estimate at best, it should be worked out as accurately as possible. And because it will usually be scrutinized by trained accountants when it reaches the foundation, be sure to prepare it as professionally as possible. If you are weak in the art of financial presentation, find a qualified person to help you.

The degree of financial detail you include in your budget will depend on the foundation and on the type of project for which you are seeking funds. In general, try to be as specific as possible. Foundation executives are quicker to find fault with vague figures than with excessive detail. But don't bore the executive. One to two pages of single-spaced copy, depending upon the complexity of the project, is ample for the budget.

Your choice of format will also depend on the foundation's preferences (if any are indicated) and on the nature of your project. Unless you have your own favorite format, we suggest that you use these nine categories as a starting point:

PERSONNEL

OUTSIDE SERVICES

RENT

UTILITIES

EQUIPMENT

SUPPLIES

TRAVEL and MEETINGS

MISCELLANEOUS EXPENSES

GENERAL RESERVE

Each of these nine categories is discussed later in this budget section, and each is also illustrated in the Sample Proposal to be found in Part Four of this book.

Adjust our suggested nine-category budget format to suit your particular situation. For instance, if your sub-category for printing material is exceptionally large, create a separate category for it. The converse is true too. For example, if your "Travel and Meetings" dollar total does not warrant a separate category, include these expenses within your "Miscellaneous" category.

How large in dollars should your budget be? The best advice is to be as realistic as possible. A skimpy budget can be just as self-defeating as a padded one. On the subject of budget padding, there is a school of thought that advocates, "Inflate your budget, since it will probably be cut anyway." Don't heed this counsel because the vast majority of foundations don't automatically pare budgets. Besides, foundation executives are experts in exposing cushioned budgets.

Be especially watchful of the three budget areas that most frequently wave red flags in front of the foundation official's well-trained eyes: consulting fees, salaries, and travel expenses.

Gain as much local support as possible in the form of donated services, facilities, and equipment. This support improves your chances of success because it provides the foundation with evidence that your project has community backing. Therefore, itemize in your budget all the donated resources—and single them out, perhaps with an asterisk.

When estimating the value of the donated resources, be slightly on the conservative side. Your estimates should be low enough to give a skeptical foundation executive the benefit of the doubt, but not so conservative that you are unfair to the donors. After all, your estimate may determine how large a tax deduction your donors can take.

Suppose your donations come from many different sources. Your best tack is to relegate this space-consuming information to the addendum.

If your project is to run for a period of more than one year, provide a less detailed budget for years two, three, and so on. Take into account inflationary factors.

Our final overall budget tip is to watch your arithmetic. This might seem rather elementary, but you'd be surprised how many simple mathematical errors blemish otherwise effective proposals.

Here are some specific pointers on each of the suggested budget categories:

Personnel—Of the nine budget categories, this one will almost invariably be your largest—perhaps as much as three-quarters of your entire operating budget, especially if yours is a service-performing organization. The category's chief components are wages, salaries, and various fringe benefits. You may itemize each of these payroll expenses, but it is acceptable to most foundations if you simply estimate them at 10 percent of your wages and salaries total. To determine the going rate for wages and salaries check with several local community-service organizations to ascertain their pay scales for equivalent positions. Be prepared to pay more (or less) than the going rate because numerous variables exist, including working conditions. And if your project is to last more than one year, make sure your personnel budget takes into account merit and inflation-based raises.

Outside Services—This budget category includes professional services (legal and bookkeeping, among others), consulting and general volunteer help. Don't list any donated service unless you're sure it will be performed. Reason: you're making a legally binding contract to have these services volunteered if the grant is approved. More and more foundations are asking grantees to document in their final reports that the volunteers did in fact perform their duties.

Rent—While most foundations would certainly not want you to be penny-wise, pound-foolish by working out of a sleazy, out-of-the-way office, neither would they be favorably disposed to your renting a luxuriously furnished suite in a glittering new office tower. Be your own judge as to the quality and quantity of space you need. If you think the rental costs might seem a little high to the foundation, prepare to justify your choice. To illustrate: you could include in your addendum a letter from your local real-estate board verifying that office rents are high in your particular locale. If you must pay extra for renovations, maintenance, or any other rent-related expense, include each item in the "Rent" category.

Utilities—Don't overlook telephone-installation costs. If you expect the cost of your message units and/or long-distance calls to be high, list them in separate sub-categories—and justify these calls if you feel they might be considered excessive. If the cost of gas, water, and/or electricity is part of the rent, state so and list them as "$0" in the "Utilities" category.

Equipment—This category includes office furnishings (desks, chairs, cabinets, files, curtains, etc.), office equipment (typewriters, adding machines, photocopy machines, postage meters, etc.), and any other relatively expensive physical item needed to reach your objective. This equipment can be purchased, leased, rented, donated, or borrowed. Whatever the case, include the cost or the equivalent value of each item in the budget, either individually or collectively.

Supplies—List separately your more costly supply items such as printed stationery and postage stamps. Less costly items are better listed under a "General Office Supplies" sub-category (rubber bands, Scotch tape, paper clips, pencils, plain typing and carbon paper, typewriter ribbons, and other office necessities).

Travel and Meetings—Of the various budgetary items, "Travel and Meetings" expenses should be the most detailed. This is especially true for out-of-town travel. Never lump all your expenses together as one "trip to San Francisco" if the total exceeds $100. Allay the foundation executive's suspicions of your "living high on the hog" by itemizing airfare, hotels, ground transportation, and so on. If staff members are to be reimbursed for using their own cars, give the mileage rate along with the estimated number of miles they will drive.

Miscellaneous Expenses—If an expense is relatively small and doesn't logically fit into any of the other budget categories, then list it here. Examples: insurance, dues, books, periodicals, and printing.

General Reserve—Undoubtedly you'll have unexpected expenses no matter how meticulously you plan your budget. Foundation executives recognize and accept this reality. Therefore set up a "General Reserve" category to cover contingency expenses. A good rule of thumb for determining the dollar amount of this reserve is to multiply your total itemized budget by 5 percent. Don't use a higher percentage. Otherwise you may be accused of not thoroughly thinking out your budget.

Writing "The Program's Future" Section

Omit this section in your proposal if you are seeking money for a project that does not require funding beyond the initial-grant period. Equipment and limited-duration programs are examples of this situation.

On the other hand, if your project will require future funding, you must indicate to the foundation exactly how you plan to obtain it. It is not enough to say that you will be searching for funds or will be exploring all possible avenues of support. You must outline a realistic fund-raising plan of action. Otherwise the foundation may fear that it will be throwing good money away on a half-completed program or that it will be forced to bail you out in years to come.

When mapping out your strategy for obtaining future funds, consider these alternatives:

Persuade the foundation to agree (in writing) to renew the grant if your project reaches a predetermined level of success.

Develop a detailed plan to secure funds from other foundations and government agencies.

Devise a plan to raise funds directly from local business firms, churches, and other traditional local funding sources.

Organize a campaign to solicit funds directly from the public.

Become an entrepreneur. Generate part or all of your needed funds by charging for your services, by creating a revenue-producing publication, by selling merchandise, by sponsoring a fund-raising event, to name just a few possibilities.

The "Introduction and Summary" Section

As we have already suggested, the optimum time to write your "Introduction and Summary" section is after you've drafted your "Need" through "Program's Future" sections. For pointers on writing this section turn back to page 61.

Writing the "Addendum"

The addendum is a convenient storehouse for all the information that doesn't belong in the body of your proposal, but that is, nonetheless, too important to withhold from the reader. Some of the items most frequently found in grant-seeking addenda are:

Verification and endorsement letters from experts, fellow organizations, and community leaders. You may also wish to include published quotes from well-known authorities that support your cause, even if these authorities are not aware of your organization. For example, if a medical journal reported that a researcher predicted a national TB epidemic, this quote might be used to support the need for your mobile X-ray unit.

The names of your board members and officers.

The names of key personnel who will work on the project. Include their vitae or résumés, especially if impressive.

Statistics and other facts that reinforce points made in the proposal. This supporting data can be in the form of charts, tables, or graphs.

The IRS Letter of Exemption verifying your 501 (C) (3) tax-exempt status.

Your annual report. If you have none, consider preparing a fact sheet on your organization.

Any other in-house data that might be requested or desired by the foundation. For example, your latest audited financial report, your articles of incorporation, your state certification, or a brief rundown of your organization's other projects.

Newspaper clippings and other news coverage on your organization.

Photographs or artwork depicting your activities, but only if they are persuasive. For example, if your proposal is for funds to feed undernourished children in India, then show pictures of *them,* not of your president shaking hands with the Indian ambassador. Illustrative material can also be effectively used to help the reader visualize facilities. For instance, if your project is to build a vest-pocket park, enclose an artist's rendition of the completed park teeming with people. This sketch will help create a lasting impression of your project within the foundation official's mind.

A list of your previous and current funding sources.

A list of other foundations to whom you are submitting a similar proposal.

A survey of what has happened, is happening, and is expected to happen in your field.

How many of the above addendum items you include will depend upon their length, their effectiveness, the nature of your project, and the wishes of the foundation.

Whatever the number, clearly identify and distinguish each one. Unless the addendum is very short, physically separate it from the proposal.

You have a wide choice of packaging units for your addendum. The best, in our judgment, are folders with fasteners or ring binders. These will keep the individual addendum items in the exact order in which they are referred to in the body of your proposal.

As to the name of the document, call it what you wish: "Addendum," "Appendix," or "Supporting Data." They all mean the same thing to the reader.

Writing the "Cover Letter"

Having drafted your proposal and addendum, you are ready to write your cover letter, the stage-setter for your proposal. Its core is basically a distilled version of your "Introduction and Summary" section, which is in itself a distillation of your entire proposal.

Spend time composing the letter. It's the first communication from you that the foundation will read. Not only do you want to create a favorable first impression; you also want to avoid having the nature of your project misunderstood. Foundations sometimes use the cover letter to determine how seriously they wish to examine the proposal.

Your cover letter should:

State your request.
Relate the project to the foundation's field of interest.
Tell who you are and establish your credentials.
Convey your excitement about your project.
Relate your organization to the need and to the foundation (perhaps by thanking the foundation executive for a previous meeting).
Volunteer to supply additional material.

SAMPLE COVER LETTER

Dear [Foundation Executive]:

I am pleased to enclose our proposal for a one-year grant of $50,000 to establish a new youth center for poverty-stricken children in the ABC neighborhood, our city's most depressed area.

We believe this project provides XYZ Foundation with a unique opportunity to further its goal of helping underprivileged children in Houston. The project is enthusiastically backed by our whole organization, Neighborhood Help. As you know, we were the founders of the DEF and GHI Youth Centers now flourishing in their respective neighborhoods.

For a more detailed overview of our project see the "Introduction and Summary" section of our attached proposal. I enjoyed our meetings over the past few months and found your suggestions most helpful. Please let me know if my staff and I can supplement our proposal with any additional information.

Sincerely,

Keep the letter short. One-half to one page in length should be sufficient. The better the foundation knows you, the less you need to say. Likewise, the better your "Introduction and Summary" section, the briefer your cover letter can be. Simply refer the reader to that section.

Use your organization's letterhead. Unless you have special reasons for doing otherwise, have the letter signed by the person whose name appears on the title page of the proposal. This minimizes confusion, as does keeping the dates on the cover letter and proposal consistent.

Now you have the three components of your formal presentation package: cover letter, proposal, and addendum. Your next step is to submit your presentation to the foundation.

STEP 9

Submit Your Formal Proposal

Your proposal is now neatly typed and proofed, and ready for the eyes of the foundation executive and trustees. At this stage you should know how many copies are needed and to whom they should be sent.

We mentioned in Step 7 the need to learn the exact application deadline date for submitting your formal proposal. This deadline date is crucial if you wish to avoid delays in having your proposal reviewed and voted on. Foundation boards meet only periodically—some quarterly, and others but once or twice a year. If your proposal arrives too late to be listed on their agenda, it will probably gather dust in the foundation's file until the board's next session.

If for some reason you are unable to learn the application deadline date but do know when the board meets, plan to have your proposal arrive at least one month before the board convenes.

An oft-asked question is: "Can we submit the same basic proposal to more than one foundation at the same time?" Realistically, you have to, if you have the opportunity. Your chances of success are too low to put all your eggs in one basket. Besides, the decision-making process of many foundations is glacially slow.

When making simultaneous submissions, however, protocol demands that you give each foundation the names of all other foundations receiving the same or a similar proposal.

How should the proposal be delivered? Most grant-seekers use the U.S. mail or a messenger service. However, the most effective method is personally delivering the proposal directly into the hands of the foundation executive. If you have this opportunity, use it.

If you do use the mail, most foundations will acknowledge the receipt of your proposal. Surprisingly, however, a few do not extend this courtesy even when they invited you to submit it. If you have doubts about the foundation sending you an acknowledgement letter, one suggestion is to send your proposal via certified mail, with a "return receipt request" (less expensive than registered mail and just as effective for your purposes).

Once your application is safely delivered, relax and be patient. The answer may arrive in a month or two, or it may be nearly a year in coming.

Sometimes the foundation will request more information or ask that you clarify a detail. Answer these inquiries promptly, and give no more or less than is requested.

Try to avoid the temptation to contact the foundation for a "weather report." Curiosity can sometimes impair your chances because the foundation might think that you are pressuring it. On the other hand, if a reasonable time has elapsed (a month or so) without any acknowledgment from the foundation, it would seem proper to write and ask if your proposal was received. Perhaps the only other reason to write would be to furnish new information, but be sure that such data is significant.

STEP 10

Follow-up

"Follow-up" is defined as your activity after you receive the foundation's final decision, be it affirmative or negative. It's important to your long-term grant-seeking success.

If the Answer Is "Yes"

Let's assume the morning mail brings a letter from Foundation XYZ stating, "Our Board of Trustees has voted to fund your project; enclosed is our check for $250,000." Pick yourself up off the floor and immediately start to compose a thank-you letter to the foundation—the sooner, the better. Keep it warm, not too businesslike, and briefly review your project's need and game plan, indicating how you will make your interim and final reports to the foundation.

What happens if you should receive full-funding approval from two foundations for your project? Well, it's not going to happen very often, so don't spend too much time worrying about it. If it does happen, you'll have to turn down the funding offer of one of the foundations. Your decision will be based on a number of factors, including which foundation offers your organization the best long-term funding potential and which foundation would be hurt most by your rejection.

When you do notify the "losing" foundation, suggest that it fund another project of your organization. Or ask it to set aside funds for your project's needs next year. It does no harm to try, and it just might work.

Reporting to the Foundation

In the past a few grant-seeking organizations didn't even acknowledge the funding money they received outside of signing the back of the foundation's check. This questionable practice has changed somewhat since the passage of the Tax Reform Act of 1969. This law requires that foundations keep stricter records on how their funds are being used; therefore the foundations are now insisting on more detailed reports from their recipients.

Nonetheless, some organizations still devote huge amounts of time to preparing proposals, but spend little time in giving progress reports or final reports to their generous benefactors.

Before starting to prepare your first interim report, study the approval letter closely and review previous communication with the foundation to determine what reporting procedures have been specified. If none has been suggested, plan to keep the foundation posted with:

A periodic progress report (perhaps quarterly) plus your final report. As with your formal proposal, make it specific, accurate, and candid. Admit your mistakes and tell the foundation your countermeasures. Keep the reports brief. Foundation executives are busy people too.

Relevant background material such as your annual report and news clippings on your project. But don't overload the foundation with irrelevant or secondary information.

If you think it would be beneficial, invite the foundation officials for an on-sight visit to see the funded project in operation. In general, try to involve the foundation as much as possible in your activities without relinquishing your independence.

Suppose at the end of the project you have surplus funds? Write the foundation, state this fact and suggest two alternatives: you will return the money or use the extra funds for another project, which you describe in your letter. Chances are the foundation will choose the latter option rather than complicate its own bookkeeping.

If the Answer Is "No"

Don't be discouraged. You probably knew from the beginning that the odds were against the approval of your proposal. Your master strategy was to identify your best prospects, zero in on those foundations, then rely upon the law of averages that one would give your proposal the green light.

Your first task is to write a thank-you letter. Here is one sample:

Dear [Foundation Executive]:

Thank you for considering our drug rehabilitation program for funding by your foundation.

Needless to say, we were disheartened by your board's decision because we and our community believe so strongly in the project. At the same time, we fully realize that your limited funds cannot possibly support the needs of the many worthy proposals submitted to you.

Our organization would very much like to keep in touch with you. Perhaps in the future we'll undertake another project that better meets your grant-giving policies.

Sincerely,

Always leave the door open. As we said before, policies, personnel, and happenstance may change. Many an organization has won a grant after long courting periods. We know of one Western university that hit the jackpot after ten years of patient pursuit.

Exit gracefully. Not only do you want to avoid jeopardizing your future chances with a foundation, you also want to protect and enhance your image in the foundation field. Foundation executives belong to a somewhat closely knit fraternity and are in steady communication with many of their colleagues.

Now comes the period of self-analysis. For the sake of future proposals, try to determine as best and as objectively as you can why your proposal failed. Perhaps its downfall was caused by one or more of the following:

There were too many other worthy proposals competing for the foundation's limited funds.

There was a cutback of available funds because of a stock-market decline or other unforeseen event.

Something said in your proposal, correspondence, or meetings displeased the foundation.

The foundation had a recent change in grant-making policy.

The foundation leadership changed—and out went your inside advocate.

Your formal proposal was submitted too late.

You were barking up the wrong tree from the very beginning because your project simply did not match up with the foundation's interests, grant-size or geographic scope. (In other words, you didn't do your homework.)

One possible source for the answers to the above suppositions is straight from the horse's mouth. Normally there shouldn't be any reason you can't write and ask the foundation why your proposal was rejected, providing you do it tactfully.

Long Term

Whether your grant proposal was accepted or rejected, you should reassess your long-term relations with each foundation. Which should be cultivated? Which should be assigned a lower priority?

The best funding sources for renewal and for your future projects are those sources that have funded you before. Match-ups of interest and people have already been established. Also, once a foundation funds your organization, you are in an excellent position to seek a larger grant the next time around (if the foundation has the giving power). That's one of the reasons why good reporting procedures prove profitable in the long run.

Keep up your public relations effort with the priority foundations that turned you down. Perhaps you can invite their officials for an on-sight inspection tour. Whatever you do, keep them up-to-date on all major developments relating to your project and organization.

Publicizing your grant-winning success stories is an excellent tactic because you can send the clippings to the various foundations you are cultivating. But make sure you have the grant-giving foundation's permission to use its name in news releases. Some foundations abhor publicity out of fear of being deluged with grant inquiries and applications from the general public.

PART TWO
How
Foundations
Differ

When most Americans hear the word foundation, they think in terms of behemoths like the Ford Foundation. Yet, there are approximately 25,000 foundations—no two alike.

What precisely is a foundation? No definition is universally accepted in the foundation field. Neither is there a legal definition. The Tax Reform Act of 1969 describes a foundation only in the negative terms of what it is not.

A less-than-ten-word definition, if one allows for many exceptions to the rule, might delineate a foundation as:

> "An IRS-sanctioned, non-profit,
> non-governmental entity financing
> public causes."

A lighthearted definition might be:

> "That strange corporate creature
> designed not to make money, but
> to give it away."

Of course, a grant-seeker needs to know more. Specifically, how foundations differ:

By category?
By being public or private?

By being operating or nonoperating?
By size?
By geographical characteristics?
By staff and facilities?
By public-relations policy?
By donor's motive?

Difference: Category

F. Emerson Andrews, in his 1956 book *Philanthropic Foundations,* classified private foundations into five groups:

1 General-purpose
2 Company-sponsored
3 Community
4 Family
5 Special-purpose

Most foundation observers now use this classification system. Each category might be described as follows:

1 GENERAL-PURPOSE FOUNDATIONS

These are usually the big foundations. The best-known members of this category are the:

Ford Foundation
Rockefeller Foundation
Carnegie Corporation

General-purpose foundations are sometimes also referred to as "independent" foundations because they are not closely influenced by a donor or family. Though only 400 in number, these well-endowed giants give away over half of all foundation grants. Most have broad grant-making philosophies and enjoy supporting innovative projects with far-reaching effects. The size of their individual grants is relatively large ($250,000 or even multimillion-dollar awards are not uncommon). Most general-purpose foundations have full-time administrative staffs and prestigious boards of trustees.

2 COMPANY-SPONSORED FOUNDATIONS

Approximately 1,500 company-sponsored foundations exist in this country. Three of the larger and better-known ones are:

> Alcoa Foundation
> Sears Roebuck Foundation
> United States Steel Foundation

Collectively, about 6 percent of all foundation assets are listed on the balance sheets of company-sponsored foundations. Each is legally independent of its company sponsor, but can have the same governing board, as some do. Most tend to fund causes closely related to their company's financial interests (such as a large client's favorite college or charity) and employees' interests (such as local colleges, hospitals, community funds, and youth agencies). All in all, education—especially higher education—is the major beneficiary. Religion-related organizations—take note—receive but a pittance of the total.

3 COMMUNITY FOUNDATIONS

Some 200 community foundations exist today, and their number and giving-power are expected to grow. A concise definition of a community foundation might be:

"A professionaly staffed foundation which receives money
from many local sources (including foundations, gifts and
wills) and distributes it to local causes according to the specific or general instructions of the donors."

The basic economic rationale for community foundations
is administrative efficiency. One staff does the work for
many foundations. Each community foundation is local in
scope and is governed by prominent local citizens. They
generally support a wide variety of causes because of the
broad range of donor instructions. Community-foundation
size varies from small to large. The two largest community
foundations are the Cleveland Foundation and the New York
Community Trust, each with assets of over $100 million.

4 FAMILY FOUNDATIONS

Over 20,000 family foundations exist, making this over-
whelmingly the largest foundation category. Yet they control
only about 15 percent of total foundation assets. Though
it's difficult to generalize about them (for instance, the di-
viding line between a general-purpose foundation and a
family foundation is somewhat hazy), certain common
denominators can be found. Most family foundations were
founded by a wealthy individual (or family) to distribute
charitable dollars according to the donor's wishes, often narrowly defined. The principal beneficiaries are colleges, hospitals, churches, and other local institutions favored by the
donor. Only a handful of these foundations have permanent
staffs. Administrative duties are usually handled on a part-
time basis by an outside professional, most often under the
close personal direction of the donor or family. As a result,
family foundations, relative to their larger cousins, tend to

be less formal in their operation and decision-making processes and more receptive to a personal approach from a grant-seeker.

5 SPECIAL-PURPOSE FOUNDATIONS

The key characteristic of special-purpose foundations is that they were founded (usually by a will or trust) to give money to one specific cause or locality. As a general rule their grant-making policies are narrowly defined. For example, specialized medical research at Stanford University or aid to American Indians living in Colorado. However, the specific cause can sometimes be broad, such as support of art or ecology.

Difference: Public or Private

The distinction between public and private foundations is vague, at least in the way they're defined in the "ultimate" source, the Tax Reform Act of 1969. The most important differences for a grant-seeker to know are:

The public foundation usually garners at least one-third of its money from appeals made to a reasonably large sector of the general public. Sometimes they are referred to as "public charities." The American Heart Association, the American Cancer Society, and Planned Parenthood are some well-known examples.

The private foundation secures most of its endowment and/or revenue from a limited, easily ledgered number of sources. Unlike the public foundation, the private foundation must pay a federal excise tax on investment income. In addition, a nonoperating private foundation must grant each year a minimum percentage (currently six percent) of the market value of its assets or an amount equal to its adjusted net income, whichever is larger. For further details on the Tax Reform Act of 1969 see Appendix A.

Difference: Operating or Nonoperating

In essence, an operating foundation undertakes its own projects, while a nonoperating foundation funds other organizations. The Menninger Foundation (a psychiatry-oriented institution) is an example of the former while the Ford Foundation is the prime example of the latter. Most foundations fall exclusively into the nonoperating category, the one that most concerns grant-seekers.

Difference: Size

The Ford Foundation represents the upside extreme, with about $2 billion in assets.

Some foundations have no appreciable assets. They receive their grant-making funds each year from their sponsors. If this type of foundation is corporate-sponsored, then the sum could fluctuate in step with the Dow Jones Average.

The average foundation endowment is slightly less than $1,000,000 (based on an estimated 25,000 foundations with approximately $20 billion in assets).

The size of the average grant is roughly $20,000 for foundations with assets of $10 million or more, $4,000 for foundations in the $1-to-$10-million asset range, and $2,000 for foundations with less than $1 million in assets.

Grant dollars are concentrated in the hands of the 2,500 largest foundations. Though these giants comprise only 10 percent of the foundation universe, they give away about 90 percent of all the grant monies.

Generally speaking, large foundations tend to award large grants, fund well-established organizations, and support innovative pilot projects, especially those effecting change on a national or international scale.

Small foundations, on the other hand, tend to be local in scope and narrower in their range of interests. Collectively, however, they support the full spectrum of grant needs, and are more willing to make general-purpose grants and to fund organizations without track records.

Difference: Geographical Characteristics

The Ford Foundation has given money away in all 50 states and nearly 100 countries. But this broad geographical interest is the exception to the rule because over 90 percent of all foundations are local in scope.

Another geographical characteristic is the concentration of foundation money. Roughly half of all foundation assets belong to foundations headquartered in New York, New Jersey, and Pennsylvania. However, this fact shouldn't cause undue alarm to grant-seekers residing in other states because most of these assets belong to the large, nationally oriented foundations.

Difference: Staff and Facilities

Only the large foundations have full-time administrators. In fact, there are only about 1,000 of these professionals in the country.

The Ford Foundation's payroll numbers several hundred employees and includes a good many high-salaried specialists, a $90,000+ -a-year president and a well-paid board of trustees which governs independently of the Ford family. Other large foundations are also well staffed, though on a smaller scale. As a rule of thumb, the larger the staff, the easier it is to get an appointment. Also, the larger a foundation is, the more likely it will be to deal with technical details, since it has specialists either on the payroll or on call.

Most foundations do not have this administrative capability. The average foundation has slightly less than $1 million in assets, and therefore only about $60,000 in annual income. It simply cannot afford to pay a full-time administrator. Instead, this function is performed on a part-time basis by an outside professional (usually a bank trust officer, attorney, or accountant) or sometimes by the donor or family member.

These foundations, in contrast to the well-staffed ones, are generally less formally run and more responsive to emotional/personal appeals and insider contact.

Another personnel-related factor worth noting is that foundation administrators and trustees differ in function and (usually) in background:

The administrator (in addition to day-to-day management duties) screens proposals, interviews applicants, conducts investigations, and makes recommendations to the Board of Trustees. In many cases the full-time executive is a former academic administrator or educator, often in the foundation's field of interest if it has one. Some foundation top executives bring distinguished career backgrounds to their jobs. Notables include McGeorge Bundy, president of the Ford Foundation, and Dean Rusk, former president of the Rockefeller Foundation.

Trustees pass final judgment on a proposal. They rely on the analysis and recommendations of the staff, but still use their own independent decision-making processes. Some boards require a majority vote for approval, while others require a unanimous decision. Board members are principally drawn from the business, education, and professional communities. Their individual credentials usually reflect the size and scope of the foundations they represent.

Office facilities among foundations also vary considerably. Most foundations have no permanent office; they operate out of a desk drawer of their part-time administrators. Other foundations—the giants—have sprawling offices. The epitome is the Ford Foundation. Its New York-based headquarters is a multimillion-dollar, strikingly modern edifice, complete with a twelve-story glass-enclosed garden. Yet one must question this so-called extravagance in proper perspective. The construction cost represents but a minute fraction of the foundation's assets, and the building's design was intended to set an example for architects. Furthermore, the entire administrative cost of the Ford Foundation is roughly 5 percent of its total grants, a reasonable figure.

Difference: Public-relations Policy

Practically all large foundations recognize the value of maintaining good public relations. They attempt to keep citizens informed of their progress and grants through annual reports and other media.

Most small and middle-sized foundations, on the other hand, do not wish to establish dialogues with the public. They either have their funds firmly committed well into the future, or they prefer to locate grant-seekers in their own way. To answer an inquiry—or even to acknowledge it with a "thanks, but no thanks" form letter—would be, in their view, a waste of limited time and resources. This attitude is a touchy point among grant-seekers.

Difference: Donor's Motive

Why do people establish foundations? For each foundation there is a different set of answers. But one or more of the following reasons probably entered the minds of most foundation founders:

> To help others.
> To influence others.
> To support a pet project.
> To give with tax-free dollars.
> To perpetuate wealth concentration.
> To organize one's giving efficiently.
> To satisfy one's compunctions.
> To satisfy one's ego.
> To sidestep heirs.

Non-Foundation Grant Sources

In the hope of treating one subject well, we restricted the scope of this book to foundation grants. However, in addition to foundations, grant or grant-type monies can also be secured from:

Government agencies, including the National Endowment for the Arts, the National Endowment for the Humanities, the National Science Foundation, and the Department of Health, Education, and Welfare (see Appendix C).

The various State Councils of the Arts. Traditionally these organizations (primarily government-supported) have favored established symphonies and other well-entrenched institutions. For further information, write your own State Council or write the national membership organization:

> Associated Councils of the Arts
> 1564 Broadway
> New York, N.Y. 10036

Corporations (not to be confused with company-sponsored foundations) donate money directly out of current revenue and treat the donations as an expense. For a statement of their gift-giving policies write to each corporation in care of "The Office of the President." Your letter will then be directed to the appropriate department.

Membership organizations, including churches, civic clubs (such as Kiwanis, Lions, and Rotary), fraternal organizations (such as Elk and Moose), labor unions (such as AFL-CIO), and women's clubs.

Voluntary fund-raising agencies (for example, the American Cancer Society) provide money for research.

PART THREE
Tools
of the Trade

AUTHORS' NOTE   Grant-seeking research tools are broad and varied. First, there are the do-it-yourself services such as those provided by the Foundation Center. There are also a number of professional services that will assume the research chores for you. In addition, there exists a host of publications giving trade news, how-to tips, and other useful information. Part Three introduces you to them. Keep in mind that the prices and availability of these services and publications are subject to change.

Foundation Center

The Foundation Center is a not-for-profit organization founded in 1956. Its basic mission is to gather, analyze, and organize comprehensive information and statistics on philanthropic foundations and to make this data conveniently available to the public for free, or at a reasonable cost. Considering the immensity of its task, the Center performs its job surprisingly well.

The Center's services are threefold:

Publications and Computerized Files
Associates Program
Libraries and Regional Collections

Though supported mainly by grants from some of the larger foundations, the Center remains independent and is governed by a board of trustees comprising leaders from both within and outside the foundation field.

Publications and Computerized Files

The *Foundation Directory* and the *Foundation Grants Index* are the two best-known and most widely used of the Center's publications. These two books, as well as the computerized files, are described later.

Associates Program

For $150 per year, individuals and nonprofit organizations may become Foundation Center Associates. As an associate, you can take advantage of the following special services that are not available to the general public:

Telephone Reference Service—The Center's staff will answer your telephone queries, providing your questions are the quick "look up" variety. This service is free.

Mail Service—If a telephone call is inconvenient or if your query requires more than a quick "look up," you can mail in your request. You'll receive a written reply free of charge, unless a photocopy or other out-of-pocket expense is necessary.

Copying Service—Associates may receive by mail the IRS Forms 990 and 990-AR on aperture cards—and photocopies of published annual reports, news clippings, and other information collected by the Center. Costs are 90¢ for the first card or page, 45¢ for each additional one. Standard-sized Data Sheets are also available on those foundations that do not publish annual reports (cost: $4 each).

Custom Searches—You may order custom computer searches of the Foundation Center's data banks. This service is described later.

Library Research Service—The staff will undertake special research assignments for $20 per hour. The gathered information will be factual in nature. Specific recommendations on foundations will not be made.

Libraries and Regional Collections

Library facilities of the Center consist of 3 national libraries and over 50 regional libraries throughout the country.

Two of the national libraries (in New York and Washington, D.C.) are maintained by the Foundation Center itself, while the third (in Chicago) is operated by the Donors' Forum. The regional libraries are sub-units of independent public, college, and foundation libraries.

Library use is free. Naturally, however, you must pay for take-home materials such as photocopies.

Prime users of the library and its resources are grant-seekers (individuals and agencies), government officials, scholars, journalists, and foundations themselves.

New York National Library

The largest and most-used national library is located in the Center's national headquarters:

> The Foundation Center
> 888 Seventh Avenue
> New York, N.Y. 10019

The library is modern, airy, and well-equipped. It commands a twenty-sixth-floor view of Manhattan that should inspire almost any grant-aspirant. But more important, it houses the world's largest and most functional collection of foundation-related material, including:

All IRS Forms 990 and 990-AR filed by some 25,000 foundations.

Annual reports (both originals and microfilm copies) of nearly every one of the approximately 300 foundations publishing them.

Standard reference books for the grant-seeker, including the Center's *Foundation Directory* and *Foundation Grants Index*.

Numerous standard reference works from the non-foundation field that relate to the grant-seeker's research needs.

Over 30 computerized printouts on microfilm of recent grants awarded in popular-subject areas.

Nearly 1,500 books on foundations and related fields—and even more pamphlets.

Current and back issues of foundation and fund-raising trade periodicals.

News clippings, plus foundation newsletters and news releases (filed by foundation name).

Historical and statistical overview data on the industry.

Information on foreign foundations.

Card catalogues on the library's vast resources.

Equipment includes microfilm/microfiche readers, reader printers, aperture-card duplicator, and a coin-operated photocopy machine.

A professional library staff provides grant-seekers with instructions on using the library resources. In keeping with the Center's policy of nonadvocacy, the librarians will not recommend foundations or tell you how to approach them. That's your job. Neither will any member of the Center's staff pave your path, let alone open the door to any foundation.

The New York library is open from 10 A.M. to 5 P.M. daily, except holidays. During the summer, library hours may change, so check with the librarian by phone before dropping by in that vacation-prone season.

Washington, D.C., National Library

The Washington, D.C., national library offers basically the same material and services as the New York library, but on a less comprehensive scale. It is run by Foundation Center personnel. Frequent users include staff members from Congress and government agencies, an indication of the factual nature of the Center's collected data. The address of this library is:

> The Foundation Center
> 1001 Connecticut Avenue, N.W.
> Washington, D.C. 20036

Chicago National Library

Because the Chicago national library is not operated, staffed, or budgeted by the Foundation Center, it cannot offer the grant-seeker all the personalized services available in the New York or Washington, D.C., libraries. Yet it still contains the hard-to-find complete set of all pertinent data, including IRS Forms 990 and 990-AR, annual reports, and the basic grant-seeker-oriented reference books. The address of the Chicago National Library is:

> The Donors' Forum
> 208 South La Salle Street
> Chicago, Illinois 60604

Regional Libraries

The more than 50 regional libraries are under the roof and control of their respective sponsoring institutions: public, college, or foundation libraries. They possess the standard foundation field reference books, annual reports, computerized printouts on microfilm of grants awarded in popular-subject areas. In addition these satellite libraries have the most recently available IRS Forms 990 and 990-AR of those foundations headquartered in their respective states or sometimes in nearby states. Consult the following list to find the regional office nearest to you. Since the Foundation Center continuously adds new regional libraries, it may be worth your while to write the Center's New York headquarters for its most current list.

State	Name	Geographical Coverage
Alabama	Birmingham Public Library 2020 Seventh Avenue, North Birmingham 35203	Alabama
Arkansas	Little Rock Public Library Reference Department 700 Louisiana Street Little Rock 72201	Arkansas
California	University Research Library Reference Department University of California Los Angeles 90024	Alaska, Arizona, California, Colorado, Hawaii, Nevada, Utah
	San Francisco Public Library Business Branch 530 Kearny Street San Francisco 94108	Alaska, California, Colorado, Hawaii, Idaho, Montana, Nevada, Oregon, Utah, Washington, Wyoming
Colorado	Denver Public Library Sociology Division 1357 Broadway Denver 80203	Colorado
Connecticut	Hartford Public Library Reference Department 500 Main Street Hartford 06103	Connecticut Massachusetts Rhode Island
Florida	Jacksonville Public Library Business, Science, and Industry Department 122 North Ocean Street Jacksonville 32202	Florida
	Miami-Dade Public Library Florida Collection 1 Biscayne Boulevard Miami 33132	Florida

State	Name	Geographical Coverage
Georgia	Atlanta Public Library 126 Carnegie Way, N.W. Atlanta 30303	Alabama, Florida, Georgia, Kentucky, Mississippi, North Carolina, South Carolina, Tennessee, Virginia
Hawaii	Thomas Hale Hamilton Library Social Science Reference 2550 The Mall Honolulu 96822	California, Hawaii, Oregon, Washington
Iowa	Des Moines Public Library 100 Locust Street Des Moines 50309	Iowa
Kansas	Topeka Public Library Adult Services Department 1515 West Tenth Street Topeka 66604	Kansas
Kentucky	Louisville Free Public Library Fourth and York Streets Louisville 40203	Kentucky
Louisiana	New Orleans Public Library Business and Science Division 219 Loyola Avenue New Orleans 70140	Louisiana
Maine	Center for Research and Advanced Study University of Maine at Portland-Gorham 246 Deering Avenue Portland 04102	Maine
Maryland	Enoch Pratt Free Library 400 Cathedral Street Baltimore 21201	Maryland
Massachusetts	Associated Foundation of Greater Boston One Boston Place, Suite 948 Boston 02108	Connecticut, Maine, Massachusetts, New Hampshire, Rhode Island, Vermont
	Boston Public Library Copley Square Boston 02117	Massachusetts

State	Name	Geographical Coverage
Michigan	Henry Ford Centennial Library 15301 Michigan Avenue Dearborn 48126	Michigan
	Grand Rapids Public Library Sociology and Education Department Library Plaza Grand Rapids 49502	Michigan
Minnesota	Minneapolis Public Library Sociology Department 300 Nicollet Mall Minneapolis 55401	Iowa, Minnesota, North Dakota, South Dakota
Mississippi	Jackson Metropolitan Library 301 North State Street Jackson 39201	Mississippi
Missouri	Kansas City Public Library 311 E. 12th Street Kansas City 64106	Kansas, Missouri
	The Danforth Foundation Library 222 South Central Avenue St. Louis 63105	Iowa, Kansas, Missouri, Nebraska
Nebraska	Omaha Public Library 1823 Harney Street Omaha 68102	Nebraska
New Hampshire	The New Hampshire Charitable Fund One South Street Concord 03301	New Hampshire
New Jersey	New Jersey State Library Reference Section 185 West State Street Trenton 08625	New Jersey
New York	New York State Library State Education Department Education Building Albany 12224	New York
	Buffalo and Erie County Public Library Lafayette Square Buffalo 14203	New York
	Levittown Public Library Reference Department 1 Bluegrass Lane Levittown 11756	New York

State	Name	Geographical Coverage
	Rochester Public Library Business and Social Sciences Division 115 South Avenue Rochester 14604	New York
North Carolina	William R. Perkins Library Duke University Durham 27706	North Carolina
Ohio	The Cleveland Foundation Library 700 National City Bank Building Cleveland 44114	Michigan, Ohio, Pennsylvania, West Virginia
Oklahoma	Oklahoma City Community Foundation 1300 North Broadway Oklahoma City 73103	Oklahoma
Oregon	Library Association of Portland Education and Psychology Department 801 S.W. Tenth Avenue Portland 97205	Alaska, California, Hawaii, Oregon, Washington
Pennsylvania	The Free Library of Philadelphia Logan Square Philadelphia 19103	Delaware, New Jersey, Pennsylvania
	Hillman Library University of Pittsburgh Pittsburgh 15213	Pennsylvania
Rhode Island	Providence Public Library Reference Department 150 Empire Street Providence 02903	Rhode Island
South Carolina	South Carolina State Library Reader Services Department 1500 Senate Street Columbia 29211	South Carolina
Tennessee	Memphis Public Library 1850 Peabody Avenue Memphis 38104	Tennessee
Texas	The Hogg Foundation for Mental Health The University of Texas Austin 78712	Arkansas, Louisiana, New Mexico, Oklahoma, Texas

State	Name	Geographical Coverage
	Dallas Public Library History and Social Sciences Division 1954 Commerce Street Dallas 75201	Texas
Utah	Salt Lake City Public Library Information and Adult Services 209 East Fifth Street Salt Lake City 84111	Utah
Vermont	State of Vermont Department of Libraries Reference Services Unit 111 State Street Montpelier 05602	New Hampshire, Vermont
Virginia	Richmond Public Library Business, Science and Technology Department 101 East Franklin Street Richmond 23219	Virginia
Washington	Seattle Public Library 1000 Fourth Avenue Seattle 98104	Washington
West Virginia	Kanawha County Public Library 123 Capitol Street Charleston 25301	West Virginia
Wisconsin	Marquette University Memorial Library 1415 West Wisconsin Avenue Milwaukee 53233	Illinois, Indiana, Iowa, Michigan, Minnesota, Ohio, Wisconsin
Wyoming	Laramie County Community College Library 1400 East College Drive Cheyenne 82001	Wyoming

Other Libraries

Foundation Center reference books and materials can also be found in the reference sections of a growing number of public and college libraries. Check with these institutions if a national or regional Foundation library is inaccessible.

Your Own Foundation Center Library

Better yet, if you can afford it, start your own Foundation Center library. Your investment could range from having just the *Foundation Directory* and *Foundation Grants Index* all the way up to a sophisticated satellite library containing microfilm data on all foundations offering funding potential for your particular project.

Foundation Center Booklet

The Foundation Center has prepared a descriptive booklet on its materials and services, entitled *Finding Foundation Facts: A Guide to Information Sources.* It can be picked up free at any Foundation Center national or regional library, or it can be obtained by writing the Center's New York library.

Foundation

Directory

Every industry has its unofficial bible and the foundation field is no exception. The *Foundation Directory* deserves this accolade, at least in the opinion of most professional grant-seekers. The book's value is further demonstrated by the fact that a librarian from the New York Public Library rated it among "the reference books most often stolen."

Foundation Directory Edition #5 gives vital information on about 2,500 of the country's largest foundations. To be included in the book, a foundation must either have at least $1 million in assets or have awarded at least $500,000 in grants during the year of record.

The bulk of the *Directory* is devoted to detailing on a state-by-state basis information about these large American foundations. Each separate foundation entry contains many, and sometimes all, of the following facts:

Name and address of the foundation.
Type of foundation.
Year and state of incorporation.
Donor(s).
Financial data, including:

Fiscal year of record.

Total assets, and whether market or book value.

Total gifts received.

Total expenditures (grants plus administrative expenses).

Total dollar amount and number of grants awarded.

Personnel, including:

Officers.

Trustees, directors, managers or governors.

Distribution committee.

Trustee bank(s).

Names of person(s) to whom your letter of inquiry should be sent (these names are italicized).

Here are several sample entries (with the foundation names and addresses disguised):

ABC Foundation
100 Main Street
Any Town, U.S.A.

Incorporated in 1945.

Donors: Avondale Mills, Comer-Avondale Mills, Inc., Cowikee Mills.

Purpose and Activities: Grants mainly to organizations in Alabama, principally for education, community funds, and recreation; some support for youth agencies and health agencies.

Financial Data (year ended 31 December 1968): Assets, $3,209,050 (M); gifts received, $172,925; expenditures, $213,281, including $206,144 for 136 grants.

Officer and Trustees: J. Craig Smith, Chairman; Donald Comer, Jr., John C. Persons.

DEF Foundation
200 Main Street
Any Town, U.S.A.

Incorporated in 1963.

Donor: W. Houston Blount.

Purpose and Activities: Charitable purposes; primarily local giving, with emphasis on higher education and community funds.

Financial Data (year ended 28 February 1970): Assets, $212,554 (L); expenditures, $41,100 for 20 grants.

Officers and Directors: W. Houston Blount, President and Treasurer; Winton M. Blount III, Secretary; A. J. Paddock.

GHI Foundation
300 Main Street
Any Town, U.S.A.

Established in 1965.
Donor: Sam M. Chappell.
Purpose and Activities: Primarily local giving, with emphasis on health agencies, hospitals, care of the aged, and education.
Financial Data (year ended 31 December 1968): Assets, $5,593 (L); gifts received, $44,400; expenditures, $41,825, including $39,325 for about 40 grants.
Officers and Directors: Sam M. Chappell, President; Percy W. Brower, Jr., Vice-President; Walter H. Brown.

The second most important section of the book consists of four indexes:

"Field of Interest"
"Donors, Trustees and Administrators"
"Foundations"
"Geographical"

All four indexes refer you to the precise page location by a page-entry number. To illustrate, "214-3" translates as the third foundation entry beginning on page 214 of the *Directory.*

Over 600 key words and phrases describing the grants are referenced in the "Field of Interest" index. However, this subject index does not include the following foundation types:

Family-funded foundations with well-entrenched local personal giving patterns (to churches, nearby colleges, etc.).
Company-sponsored foundations with firmly established policies of funding in the fields of health, education, and welfare.
Community foundations, which as a rule award grants to local organizations or make decisions based upon the donor's specific instructions.

Neither is the "Field of Interest" index comprehensive in scope—or even reasonably so. It lists only a fraction of the some 2,500 foundations detailed in the main section. Don't depend on this index for more than a representative indication of what is contained in the composite directory entries. If your project is local in scope, study the "Purpose and Activities" paragraph for each foundation listed in your geographic area in the book's main section.

"Donors, Trustees and Administrators," the second index, is sometimes helpful in determining whether a friendly or not-so-friendly trustee has decision-making influence with more than one foundation that might be potential funding sources for your particular project. This index can also help you determine whether you need to be especially cautious in making a proposal to two seemingly unrelated foundations. (The same trustee might sit on both boards and view your proposal as a carbon copy.)

While the *Directory* is undeniably an outstanding research tool, you should be aware of what it does not provide:

The *Directory* lists only 10 percent of all grant-making foundations. (However, the 2,500 that are listed disperse 90 percent of all grant money. And virtually all those that did not make the *Directory* are primarily local in scope and therefore should be researched through the Foundation Center's regional libraries.)

Specifics on each individual grant such as amount, recipient, and purpose are not given. (To find this information you must use the *Foundation Directory* in conjunction with other published sources including the *Foundation Grants Index,* annual reports, and the IRS Forms 990 and 990-AR.)

Much of the information is based on 1972 data. (However, updated information is contained in the *Foundation Directory*

Supplement, in the *Foundation Grants Index,* and in the most currently available IRS Forms 990 and 990-AR. In addition, some of the information published in *Edition #5* is based on 1973 and 1974 data volunteered by a small percentage of the foundations.)

As a means of keeping the *Foundation Directory* as current as possible, the Center also publishes its semiannual *Foundation Directory Supplement.* While it does not contain updated entries per se, the *Supplement* has an index of those revised and newly listed foundations whose descriptive listings can be purchased from the Center on microfiche cards. Each is a 4" × 6" microfilm sheet containing up to 98 pages of copy, with a reduction ratio of 24:1.

The *Supplement* also gives:

The list of foundations whose annual reports can be purchased from the Center at $2.00 per microfiche.

A bibliography of recent publications on foundation philanthropy.

An annual list of the approximately 25,000 foundations filing IRS Forms 990 and 990-AR.

The cost of the *Foundation Directory* is $30 and includes the first four *Supplements* (July 1975, December 1975, July 1976, and December 1976). Individual issues of the Supplement run $3.50 each.

To order, write to the book's distributor:

> Columbia University Press
> 136 South Broadway
> Irvington-on-Hudson, New York 10533

Foundation Grants Index

The *Foundation Grants Index,* an annual reference book, lists and cross-references nearly 10,000 grants of $5,000 or more reported from some 250 major foundations. This 9″ × 11″, several-hundred-page hardcover book is a vital tool for the grant-seeker because it:

Gives specific information on each grant.
Provides three indexes, cross-referencing the grants by subject, recipient, and foundation.
Suggests recent giving patterns of each foundation and of foundations in general.

The book is divided into four sections:

"Section I—Grants."
"Section II—Recipients."
"Section III—Key Words & Phrases."
"Section IV—Foundations."

Section I comprises about 75 percent of the book and lists grant-making foundations alphabetically by their state location. Under each foundation name you'll find the individual grant records arranged alphabetically by recipient. Basic information includes, in order:

Grant size.

Recipient name and location.

Grant authorization date.

Grant description (in most cases).

Grant identification number (for cross-reference purposes).

Some of the grant records in Section I provide still more data under this coding system:

RT = Type of recipient.

PG = Population group to receive benefit from the activity.

PH = Phase of activity.

LO = Site(s) of activity other than recipient location.

LM = Program, geographic or other limitation set by the foundation.

SD = Source of grant data.

Here are some sample Section I listings:

XYZ FOUNDATION
$20,000 to **Easter Seal Society,** Hemlocks, The, Hartford, CT. 2/9/73. To build new facilities for the physically handicapped in the State of Connecticut. The new facility will be a year-round residence, recreational and educational center *RT:* Health *PG:* Those afflicted with orthopedic and crippling disorders *PH:* Operation *SD:* 2/26/73 FF   **(3071)**

$20,000 to **Institute of Living,** Audio-Visual Education Program Department, Hartford, CT. 2/9/73. To evaluate the Institute's present audio-visual program and to assist in expansion and reorganization of the Institute's information, education and training program. The grant makes provision for video-tape hardware, audio-visual technician, video-tape and video consultant. Emphasis will be on incorporating existing hardware with new acquisitions, the development of software, and a needs and application assessment *RT:* Mental Health *PG:* Mentally or emotionally disturbed *PH:* Operation *SD:* 2/22/73 FF   **(3072)**

$47,500 to **New York State Coalition for Family Planning,** Video-Communications Project, NYC, NY. 2/9/73. To further the application of video cassette technology as a basic means of communication. The major aspects of this program relate to (1) programming the software for video cassette application (2) content identification of programming areas (3) an appropriate network system for distribution *RT:* Population *PG:* Community members *PH:* Operation *SD:* 2/22/73FF   **(3073)**

$11,000 to **Planned Parenthood League of Connecticut,** Clinics, New Haven, CT. 2/9/73. For contraceptive education, information and counseling for women and men in need or desiring family planning information. Part of the funds will be applied to an information/education program on a pilot basis using video-tape technology *RT:* Population *PH:* Operation *SD:* 2/26/73 FF   **(3074)**

"Section II—Recipients," is an index listing recipient names along with grant identification numbers, allowing you to find quickly and easily the appropriate grant records in Section I. It is divided into two parts, domestic and foreign recipients, in that sequence. Below are some sample Section II listings.

A Better Chance, MA *1127 2734 3397 6409*
A Better Chance, NY *794 2239 4081*
A Better Chance, OH *6609 6640*
A Better Chance—National Public Schools, NJ *2733*
Abbott House, NY *5601*
Abilene Christian College, TX *5493 7734*
Abilene Philharmonic Association, TX *7770*
Absalom Jones Theological Institute, GA *3182*
Academix Incorporated, MA *6410*
Academy for Educational Development, NY *1477 4082 6116*
Academy of Natural Sciences of Philadelphia, PA *6931*
Academy of the New Church, PA *6932*
Accion International, NY *5602 6321*
Accounting Aid, Inc., MA *1478*
Action for Children's Television, MA *4083*
Action Planning Council, TX *7723*
Action-Housing, Inc., PA *7117 7373*
Ada S. McKinley Community Services, IL *1178*

Adams-Morgan Community Council, DC *571*
Adelphi University, NY *6158*
Administrative and Management Research Association of the City of New York, NY *5810*
Adrian College, MI *1819 2090*
Adult Education Tutorial Program, CO *323*
Affiliate Artists, Inc., NY *3207*
Affiliated Hospitals Center, MA *1414 1432 1455*
African Cultural Center, NY *5811*
African Free School, NJ *2735*
African Medical and Research Foundation, NY *795 1820*
African Peoples Theatre, CA *172*
African Student Aid Fund, NY *6411*
African Wildlife Leadership Foundation, NY *5603*
African-American Institute, NY *3309 3310 3398 5604 5605 5812*
Afro-American Family and Community Services, IL *1179*
Afro-American Federation, PA *7191*
Afro-American Total Theatre Arts Foundation, NY *5606*

"Section III—Key Words & Phrases," is an index designed to help you find funded projects similar to yours. Since there are a number of categories under which a grant can be listed, it is a good idea to check through the entire "Key Words & Phrases" index for every possible topic heading. For example, if you were seeking funds for a birth-control project, you would find the key words and phrases "population" and "family planning" as well as "birth control." Once having found the appropriate listings, the grant identification number will quickly refer you to the full grant description in Section I. Here are some sample Section III entries:

Abilities prediction, black students 6458
Abortion and family planning 3677
Abortion counseling & service 3059
Abortion information 5621
Abortion information-youth clinics 79
Abortion, civil rights 6278
Academic administration, internships 5847
Academic curriculum revision 7829
Academic disputes, computer use 3313
Accounting aid, nonprofit 1478
Accounting instruction-experimental project 6199
Acoustical technology 5963
Acquisition fund, art 2276
Acquisitions, law library 118 138
Acupuncture research, laboratory animals 6916
Acupuncture research, pain technician 6916
Addiction (drug), interagency communication 5339
Addiction prevention 748 833
Addicts (former), business support 4605
Administration of criminal justice 1065
Administration training, hospital 3849
Administration, community college 3946

Administration, health 3865
Administrative & business education, Thailand 4379
Administrative advancement, academic women 3388
Administrative internship 6426
Administrative internships (college & university) 3338
Administrators (school), training 5914
Administrators, health sciences 1668
Admissions, open 1131
Adolescent psychiatry, cross-cultural 4706
Adopted children (schizophrenic), study 4749
Adoption 4693
Adoption (child) 2376 2884
Adoption-research programs 7242
Adoption council, Episcopal mission 3572
Adoption exchange 5367
Adoption information 7209
Adoption program 3573
Adoption program (national) 3183
Adoption service (black) 6630
Adoption services 2962
Adoption services-support 2883
Adoption services, children 2829
Adult development, analysis 4757
Adult education 323

"Section IV—Foundations," is an index of foundation names cross-referenced to Section I by page number.

Although the primary source of the data published in the *Foundation Grants Index* is direct reporting from foundations to the Foundation Center, the book must also rely upon indirect sources such as annual reports, IRS Form 990-ARs, news clippings, and press releases. Another limitation of the *Foundation Grants Index:* it is by no means comprehensive.

Despite these limitations, the *Foundation Grants Index* is

easily the best and most complete published source of its kind available. That's why so many professional grant-seekers regard it as one of their indispensable tools.

The *Foundation Grants Index* costs $15. Write to its distributor:

> Columbia University Press
> 136 South Broadway
> Irvington-on-Hudson, New York   10533

If your budget is low, check first with your local library to see if it has a copy on its lending or reference shelves.

Foundation Grants Index—Bimonthly Edition

Between annual publication dates of the *Foundation Grants Index* book, the Foundation Center keeps grant-seekers current by preparing special *Bimonthly* editions of new grants. These computer-based documents are published as a removable center section of the six-times-a-year *Foundation News* magazine (described later on page 141).

Each magazine insert contains records of over 1,000 newly reported grants of at least $5,000 magnitude. At the end of the year, the six issues are combined and become the following year's *Foundation Grants Index* book.

You can buy the *Bimonthly* editions only by purchasing the *Foundation News*. A one-year subscription runs $15 (only $10 for foundations). To order write the magazine's publisher:

> Council on Foundations
> 888 Seventh Avenue
> New York, New York   10019

Since each latest *Foundation Grants Index* book covers only the grants reported during its preceding year, it is a sound idea to back-order your initial *Foundation News* subscription to the beginning of the calendar year to ensure a continuous record of all reported grants.

Foundation Center Computerized Search

Foundation Center Associates (see page 104) can custom order a computer printout by foundation or grant category by taking advantage of the Foundation Center's extensive data banks. These computerized retrieval records include:

Detailed data on 2,500 large foundations (based on information from the *Foundation Directory Edition #5* Data Bank). Facts include:

Foundation Name	Highest Grant Amount
Former Name	Lowest Grant Amount
Care of (Name)	Program Amount
Street	No. of Programs
City	Matching Gifts Amount
State	No. of Matching Gifts
Zip Code	Scholarship Amount
Establishment Data	No. of Scholarships
Donor Name(s)	Loan Amount
Purpose and Activities	No. of Loans
Asset Amount	Names & Titles of Officers
Asset Type (Market or Book)	and Trustees
Gifts Received	Fields of Interest
Expenditures	Limitations
Grants Amount	Foundation Type
No. of Grants	IRS Employer Identification No.

Less detailed data on 25,000 foundations, with a stress on financial information (based on information from the *Foundation Directory Edition #5* Regional Data Bank). Facts include:

Foundation Name
IRS Employer
Identification No.
Year of Tax Exemption
Letter
Care of (Name)
Street
City
State
Zip
Fiscal Year Date of Tax Return

Total Assets
(Market or Book)
Total Contributions
No. of grants given
Highest grant
Lowest grant
Name and Title of Principal Officer
Final Return Indicator
Gifts received
Gross Income

All grants (minimum $5,000 in size) reported in the *Founda-dation Grants Index* Data Bank, beginning with 1972. Facts include:

Foundation Name
Foundation State
Recipient Organization
Unit of Recipient Organization
Type of Organization
Recipient City
Recipient State/Country
Full Amount Authorized
Date of Authorization
Duration of Funding

Description of Grant
Population Group to Receive
Benefit
Phase of Activity
Site(s) of Activity Other Than
Recipient Location
Program, Geographic, or Other
Limitations
Sources of Further Information

All grants (regardless of size) reported by the 2,500 foundations listed in the *Foundation Directory Edition #5* Data Bank. Facts include:

Foundation Name
IRS Employer Identification No.
Recipient's Name
City

State and Country
Grant Amount
Text (sometimes detailed)

Suppose you want to extract from the computer those specific grants related to your project. This task will not be all that difficult, even if you have never communicated with a computer before.

Simply put, you will ask the computer to print out a list of grants based on key words or phrases you select. For example, if you were seeking foundation funds for a "76 Trombone Band," you could instruct the computer to retrieve all grant records containing the key words "**band**" and "orchestras"—to name just two possibilities. "Music" as a key word would be too broad, while the words "trombone" or "brass" would probably yield few, if any, grant records.

Your computerized search can also be based upon other criteria such as:

Geographical location ("Funding from Massachusetts").
Recipient name ("Grants received by Boston Symphony").
Foundation name ("Grants awarded by XYZ Foundation").
Size of grant ("$25,000 or more").

Better yet, zero in on your target by instructing the computer to use a combination of two or more of these criteria.

Since the Foundation Center feeds new grant information into the computer almost as fast as it is received, the data banks are more current and comprehensive than the *Foundation Grants Index* book. Still another benefit: you can receive the data in the format of your choosing. For example, you can have the grants arranged alphabetically by state locations of foundations or recipients, by name of foundation or recipient, and/or by grant size.

The cost for a computer search of the *Foundation Directory Edition #5* Data Bank is $85 per hour (minimum charge $45). If your key words or phrases are broad, or if your budget is skimpy, you should prudently consider placing a limit on the number of grant records you wish to receive. Allow two or three weeks for processing and delivery.

Standard Subject Lists

The Foundation Center has ready-to-use grant listings on microfiche cards in over 30 broad categories of popular interest. They are grouped below by field.

Arts and Cultural
Visual Arts
Music
Dance & Theater
Museums
Historical Projects
The Media
Education
Elementary & Secondary Education
Educational Administration & Research
Scholarships & Fellowships
Libraries
Health
Medical Education
Medical Research
Hospitals
Mental Health
Physical Sciences
Chemistry & Physics
Agriculture & Biology
Environmental Programs
Religion
Theological Education
Churches & Temples
Social Sciences
Psychology & Sociology
Business & Economics
Government & Politics
Law & Justice
Welfare & Social Concerns
Child Welfare
Youth Agencies
The Handicapped
The Aged
Minorities
Crime & Delinquency
Community Development
Alcohol & Drug Abuse

Each subject (for example, "Visual Arts") contains from 100 to 1,000 individual grant records arranged by state location of the foundation. Each individual grant record includes the name of the foundation, the grant amount, name and location of the recipient, and in most cases a description of the grant's purpose.

You may purchase these standard subject lists directly

from the Foundation Center's New York office on microfiche cards at $3 to $12 per subject.

Or, you may examine the microfiche and/or paper copies free of charge at any of the Foundation Center's national or regional libraries.

Annual Reports

Some 300 foundations publish annual reports. Generally, these are the large, well-staffed national foundations.

The values of a published annual report to a grant-seeker are several:

The latest annual report is more current—often by over one year—than the IRS Forms 990 and 990-AR aperture cards issued by the government.

The annual report usually gives a brief description of each grant awarded, including the amount, recipient, and purpose. This information is critical in assessing recent grant patterns.

Most annual reports provide the grant-seeker with the foundation's history and philosophy, operating and application procedures, financial and personnel data, among other useful information.

You can obtain published annual reports in two ways: from the Foundation Center on microfiche cards, or directly from the foundations you are researching.

The Foundation Center has reproduced virtually all the available published annual reports on microfiche. These can be examined free of charge at any of the Foundation Center's national or regional libraries.

You can also purchase the microfiches individually ($2

per foundation) or in sets (prices vary from $4 to $25 per set). Write:

The Foundation Center
888 Seventh Avenue
New York, New York 10019

Tabletop microfiche viewers are available at most large college or public libraries. Hand-held viewers can usually be purchased from a local retail store. Look in your classified telephone book under the subject heading "Microfilm" —or ask your local camera shop if it can order a hand-held viewer for you.

Writing directly to the foundation is the second way to secure an annual report. This method requires a clerical chore as well as postage stamps, but is usually worthwhile because you gain the latest data available to the public.

IRS Forms 990 and 990-AR

Thanks to the Tax Reform Act of 1969, grant-seekers can gain vital data on any of the approximately 25,000 private foundations. This information is found on the IRS Forms 990 and 990-AR that all private foundations are required to file annually with the Internal Revenue Service. These documents are public record, and anyone can examine or purchase them.

Basically the IRS Form 990 is the information return filed by all private foundations, while the Form 990-AR serves as an annual report for the 99 percent of foundations which do not publish one.

There is one drawback: due to the IRS filing cycle and processing system, the 990 and 990-AR documents are not available to the public until they are 1½ to 2 years old. Keep this fact in mind when extracting information from the forms.

The IRS Form 990-AR is far more valuable to the grant-seeker than the IRS Form 990 because it includes the following pertinent information on each foundation:

Name and address of the foundation.
Names, titles, and business addresses of the foundation's chief executive, manager, and trustees.

Financial data on the foundation's:
  Assets, investments, and revenues.
  Expenses.
  Grant amounts and recipients.
  Grant descriptions (in many cases).

The IRS Form 990-AR is especially essential for researching smaller foundations. (Historically, most have not been eager to volunteer information to inquiring grant-seekers.)

The IRS Forms 990 and 990-AR are published by the Internal Revenue Service on aperture cards. These are ordinary computer punch cards mounted with a microfilm containing up to 15 filmed pages, one for each page of the original IRS Forms 990 and 990-AR. Most foundation returns fit on no more than two aperture cards.

These aperture cards may be purchased directly from the Internal Revenue Service. Cost: $1.00 for the first card, 10¢ for each additional one. You may order as few as one and as many as the entire nation set (which runs over $5,000). Write:

> Director
> Internal Revenue Service
> P.O. Box 187
> Cornwells Heights, Pennsylvania   19020

When placing your order, you must identify each foundation by the exact name appearing on the IRS aperture card, along with its city and state location. To determine these specifics, consult a July issue of the *Foundation Directory Supplement*.

Allow several weeks (sometimes longer) for delivery of the aperture cards from the Internal Revenue Service.

The aperture cards may be also purchased by mail from the Foundation Center, providing you are an Associate and you are not bulk ordering. Costs are 90¢ for the first card, 45¢ for each additional card. The public may duplicate the cards at the same price while visiting the Foundation Center's libraries in New York or Washington, D.C.

If you don't have a microfilm viewer, you might use the one in your local library. If a viewer is unavailable, or if you expect to be using one frequently, you can purchase a hand-held viewer from a local retail shop (look under "Microfilm" in your local classified directory or check with your local camera store).

Another option, if you are a Foundation Center Associate, is to order full-size paper copies called Data Sheets at $4 per foundation from the Foundation Center. This method will be costly if you are researching a number of foundations. And Data Sheets are usually not available for the 300 large foundations publishing regular annual reports.

You can examine the IRS aperture cards or copies free of charge by visiting:

The Foundation Center's national and regional libraries.

The Internal Revenue Service District Office whose jurisdiction includes the foundation's locale. For an appointment, write and give full details including name of documents desired, specific foundation names, and tax year. The IRS will contact you when the data is ready for examination. Allow 6 to 8 weeks.

The State Attorney General's Office in the foundation's home state. In some states the records are maintained by other agencies.

The principal office of the foundation. By law, each foundation must keep (for 180 days after it runs its official notification in the newspaper) a copy of its IRS Forms 990 and 990-AR for public review.

An actual sample of portions of an IRS Form 990-AR is reprinted in Appendix E.

Other Major Tools

Individualized Services—An Introduction

A number of organizations serve as consultants, hold seminars, provide packaged data, and/or conduct custom searches for grant-seekers in pursuit of foundation monies. The scope of their services and the size of their fees vary widely. Some are commercial enterprises while others are nonprofit organizations. Some edit publications in addition to offering individualized services. If they are reputable, they will never attempt to influence one of their foundation contacts on your behalf or guarantee that the advice or data you purchase will produce results.

The following organizations offer custom individualized services. Each is described (along with other tools) in the alphabetically arranged sections in this chapter.

Brakeley, John Price Jones
Foundation Research
Foundation Research Service
Funding Sources Clearinghouse
Grants Development Institute
Grantsmanship Center
Institute for Fund-Raising

Marts & Lundy
Public Service Materials Center
Taft Information System
T & B Public Grants Services

Names and descriptions of other large fund-raising counseling firms can be found in the "Directory of Members"
booklet of the American Association of Fund-Raising Counsel, Inc., 500 Fifth Avenue, New York, N.Y. 10036. Write
for a free copy.

Who uses these services? The users are primarily those
grant-seekers lacking sufficient time, in-house expertise, raw
material, or inclination to do the research chores. An under-
staffed office such as the development department of a small
college is therefore far more apt to hire these outside services
than is the well-staffed development department of a large
university.

These services have raised controversy in some quarters.
Their critics say they render useless and inaccurate information, do little more than the research grant-seekers should
be doing themselves, offer false hopes, and give overly-
personalized information on foundation officials.

Their advocates, on the other hand, are convinced that
using these services is far more cost-effective than doing the
research themselves. If you are after $100,000 to $500,000,
they argue, then you need all the essential facts and available time you can muster.

The key to using their services is to know precisely what
you're buying and how to interpret and use the data wisely.

American Association of Fund-raising Counsel

AAFRC is a trade organization of professional fund-raising counseling services. Members include most of the large national firms.

One of AAFRC's publications, *Giving U.S.A.—Annual Report,* is a must for any grant-aspirant seeking a statistical overview of current philanthropic trends. This $3.50 booklet is filled with charts and graphs on major donor categories (including foundation, individual, church, and corporate) and recipient categories. Write:

> American Association of Fund-Raising Counsel, Inc.
> 500 Fifth Avenue
> New York, New York 10036

You can receive a free copy of *Giving U.S.A.—Annual Report* by subscribing to the *Giving U.S.A.—Bulletin,* a monthly newsletter. The *Bulletin* gives briefs on philanthropy, updated statistics and—most important of all to the grant-seeker—a representative listing of recent donations and grants made by individuals, corporations, and foundations.

A $12.50 annual subscription for the *Bulletin* also includes a free copy of the "Master Calendar" of meetings, seminars, and conferences related to the philanthropic field.

Annual Register of Grant Support

This huge reference volume is primarily intended to serve individuals seeking scholarships, advance study awards, and research grants (see Appendix D).

Brakeley, John Price Jones

A complete service for the grant-seeker is offered by Brakeley, John Price Jones—all the way from project evaluation to grant-application strategy and proposal writing. Less extensive services are also available from this commercial firm.

The organization publishes *Philanthropic Digest*, a 16-issue-per-year newsletter reporting the details of recent grants and bequests. A subscription runs $15 per year.

For more information on the firm, or to place a subscription order for the *Digest*, write:

> Brakeley, John Price Jones, Inc.
> 6 East 43rd Street
> New York, New York 10017

Bread Game

Taking a somewhat underground approach, the $2.95, 88-page paperback, *The Bread Game*, provides general grant-seeking tips. Write the publisher:

> Glide Publications
> 330 Ellis Street
> San Francisco, California 94102

Business Directories

The business world is replete with directories detailing both companies and key personnel. Most large public libraries shelve them.

Poor's Register (the popular shortened name) is a bulky,

multi-thousand-page volume containing data on 35,000 companies plus brief biographical data on 75,000 directors and top executives. This annually revised edition can be leased (never purchased) for one year for $140. Write the publisher:

Standard & Poor's Corporation
345 Hudson Street
New York, New York   10014

Other useful business publications for researching biographical information on trustees and specific data on corporations include *Directory of Directors* and Dun & Bradstreet's *Million Dollar Directory*.

Council on Foundations

Though sharing the twenty-sixth floor with the Foundation Center at 888 Seventh Avenue in New York City, the nonprofit Council on Foundations is independent and serves a totally different function.

The Council on Foundations is a trade organization for foundations and therefore is not geared to satisfy the needs of grant-seekers. Its membership consists of some 500 general-purpose foundations plus a smaller number of community foundations, corporation foundations, and corporations with philanthropic programs void of foundation ties.

The Council publishes *Foundation News*, the now-and-then tabloid *Regional Reporter*, and a number of special booklets for its members. It also offers its membership advisory services and conducts conferences.

Foundation News

The *Foundation News,* a bimonthly magazine published by the Council on Foundations, is primarily a trade publication for foundation executives and trustees. Yet it is an essential tool for the grant-seeker as well, because it contains the detachable *Foundation Grants Index—Bimonthly* describing recently reported grants of $5,000 or more. Only through the *Foundation News* can you obtain this six-times-a-year update of the *Foundation Grants Index—Annual.*

The rest of each *Foundation News* issue contains subject matter that is, in almost all cases, low priority reading for busy grant-seekers. To illustrate:

"Are Foundations an Endangered Species?"
"Prudence and Creativity: A Trustee Responsibility"
"A Note on 19th Century Foundations"

The remaining editorial space covers trade news items: conference dates, personnel notes, book reviews, editorials, legislative and tax developments, industry trends, and other news mainly relevant to foundation executives.

A one-year subscription costs $15. Write:

Council on Foundations
888 Seventh Avenue
New York, New York 10019

Past issues dating back to September, 1960, are available from the Foundation Center on microfiche (4" x 6" microfilm sheets containing up to 98 pages of copy). These microfiche cards can be viewed free of charge at any of the Center's national or regional libraries.

Foundation Research Service

Foundation Research Service is a subsidiary of Lawson & Williams Associates, Inc., a management consulting firm. It publishes *Foundation 500,* a book detailing the country's largest foundations. Cost: $19.50.

For further information, write:

> Lawson & Williams Associates, Inc.
> 39 East 51 Street
> New York, New York 10022

Funding Sources Clearinghouse

FSC is a nonprofit organization that undertakes foundation research tasks for you. Both FSC's size and reputation are growing rapidly in the foundation field because FSC offers grant-seekers an excellent value.

Using its extensive data banks, FSC conducts custom computerized searches of foundations. An FSC staff specialist then pares down the list to the most promising 5 or 10 foundations for your particular project. You receive both the analysis and in-depth reports on each foundation.

For a $250 annual membership fee you receive:

One free project-grant search.
Additional project-grant searches at $25 each.
A free monthly digest of current grant-seeking news.
Biographical profiles on foundation officials at $1 each.
Other free and useful information such as a funding alert.

In addition, FSC will evaluate your letter proposal for $50 (nonmembers: $75) or your formal proposal for $125 (nonmembers: $200). FSC's service is available only to nonprofit organizations.

For further information, write the main office:

Funding Sources Clearinghouse, Inc.
2600 Bancroft Way
Berkeley, California 94704

Fund Raising Management

The broad sweep of fund-raising and philanthropic activities is covered by this glossy, ad-packed, bimonthly trade journal. Though it seldom has articles of vital interest to a grant-seeker, it does provide an industry-wide perspective.

One-year subscriptions run $8 each. Write the publisher:

Hoke Communications, Inc.
224 Seventh Street
Garden City, New York 11530

Grant Development Institute

The Institute publishes a loose-leaf volume for grant-seekers, entitled *A Comprehensive Guide to Successful Grantsmanship*. This book instructs grant-seekers on developing long-range fund-raising programs, researching foundation prospects, evaluating proposals, and planning application strategies. A *Grant Development Digest,* issued periodically, updates the main volume.

The Institute also conducts small seminars for organizations interested in fund-raising and grant-development programs.

For further information on the publications and seminars write:

Grant Development Institute
2525 West Main
Littleton, Colorado   80120

Grantmanship Center

The Grantsmanship Center provides a valuable service for grant-seeking organizations, especially those which have not yet developed professional grant-seeking skills and which cannot afford to use an outside research service.

Founded in 1972 as a nonprofit organization, the Grantsmanship Center offers two basic services:

The Grantsmanship Center News—This well-written tabloid newspaper is filled with how-to and other informative articles relating to the grant-seeker's specific needs. A subscription runs $15 per year. (8 issues).

Workshops—The Grantsmanship Center conducts week-long training seminars in large cities across the country. Participants, limited to 15 to 18, are nonprofit organizations lacking grant-seeking expertise. All basic phases of grant-seeking, from organization self-evaluation to proposal writing and follow-up, are covered. The workshop fee is $245.

For a subscription, or for further information on the workshops, write:

The Grantsmanship Center
P.O. Box 44759
7815 South Vermont
Los Angeles, California   90044

Grants Register

This book covers scholarships and advanced study awards for individuals (see Appendix D).

Help from within Your Field

Specialized assistance can often be obtained from the trade organizations and periodicals within your own field. For example, in the field of higher education, the American Alumni Council and the American College Public Relations Association (now merging) offer considerable published material relating to grant-seeking and fund-raising activities. Also, the Council for Financial Aid to Education publishes several useful books, including the *Handbook of Aid to Higher Education*.

Other examples of valuable specialized publications are the *Behavior Today Newsletter* (published by *Psychology Today*) and *The Catholic Guide to Foundations*.

How to Obtain Foundation Grants

Requiring 345 loose-leaf pages, this well-organized tome covers practically all aspects of grant-seeking. Detailed discussions on approach techniques, proposal writing, and follow-up are backed with sample letters, reports, and grant applications. Cost: $75. To order, or for more information, write the publisher:

> R. L. Houts Associates, Inc.
> 3960 Wilshire Boulevard
> Los Angeles, California 90010

Human Resources Network

Human Resources Network, a nonprofit firm, has re-searched and written a series of four 8½" × 11" paperback books entitled *How To Get Money For* . . . . Each pub-lication covers funding sources in different topic areas:

Book 1
Education, Scholarship, Fellowship ($5.95)
Book 2
Health, Drugs and Alcohol Abuse, and the Arts ($5.95)
Book 3
Youth, the Elderly, the Handicapped, Women and Civil Lib-erties ($7.95)
Book 4
Community Development and Conservation ($5.95)

All four books are organized according to municipal geographical locations—150 cities in all. A wide variety of fund-givers is listed: foundations, corporations, labor unions, and federal, state, and local agencies.

Each listing gives essential data such as name and address of the funding source, whom to contact, grant patterns and restrictions, and application deadlines.

Also contained in each of the four books is a "how-to" section dealing with proposal writing and approaching the funding source.

A hardcover edition containing the contents of all four paperback books runs $39.95. Write the publisher:

Chilton Book Company
Chilton Way
Radnor, Pennsylvania 19089

Institute for Fund-Raising

Two-day seminars on "Foundation and Government Grants & Proposal Preparation" are offered periodically in Chicago, Los Angeles, and New York by the Institute for Fund-Raising. Fee: $245 per person. For more details write:

> Institute for Fund-Raising
> 717 Castro Street
> San Francisco, California 94114

Magazines and Newspapers

Magazines, especially the general-business trade publications, sometimes contain articles directly or indirectly related to grant-seeking. For instance, *Fortune* annually publishes its famous "500 Directory" of the country's largest industrial firms, an excellent reference list for anyone seeking financial assistance from corporations. *Business Week* and *Forbes* are also good sources for articles on foundation and corporate giving.

The best quick-reference source for finding grant-related magazine articles is, of course, the *Reader's Guide to Periodical Literature*, found in almost any public or college library.

Newspapers now and then carry news stories and feature articles concerning foundation and corporate giving.

Marts & Lundy

The services provided by this well-established firm range from program evaluation and long-range grant development to fund-raising campaign management and public relations. For further details write:

> Marts & Lundy, Inc.
> 521 Fifth Avenue
> New York, New York 10017

National Council on Philanthropy

NCOP comes closest to being the umbrella organization for the entire field of philanthropy. Membership comprises donors from nearly all major categories (including foundation and corporate) and many key institutional recipients.

The Council's activities include the study of problems in volunteer giving, as well as research projects and national conferences. These well-planned assemblies are attended by a cross-section of key professionals from the philanthropic world, including fund-giving administrators, fund-seeking executives, and involved community leaders. Together they examine a wide variety of major issues and subjects, such as the assessment of priorities among current social problems, the effect of tax laws on volunteer giving, and the ways of improving administrative efficiency on both the part of donors and recipients.

For literature on NCOP and its next conference, write:

> National Council on Philanthropy
> 680 Fifth Avenue
> New York, New York 10019

Non-Profit Report, The Philanthropy Monthly

A monthly trade journal, the *Non-Profit Report* is primarily written for the fund-giving executives of foundations and corporations. It contains specialized articles on such topics as legislation and taxation. A special insert entitled "A Voice for Philanthropy" is written for fund-givers by the National Council on Philanthropy (see above).

Non-Profit Report gives the grant-seeker an insight into the foundation executive's current concerns and has two features which have proven useful to grant-seekers:

An annual listing of the "100 Largest U.S. Foundations Ranked by Grants."

News items in the "Fund Raising" newsletter section.

Subscriptions cost $48 per year to nonprofit grant-seeking organizations. (Regular annual subscriptions run $72.) Back issues are $2 each. Write:

> Non-Profit Report, Inc.
> 205 Main Street
> Danbury, Connecticut   06810

Private Foundation Reports

Supplemented biweekly, the two-volume *Private Foundation Reports* provides current news and analysis of federal and state laws affecting private foundations and other tax-exempt organizations.

Subscriptions are $195 for 1 year, $350 for 2. To order, or for further information, write the publisher:

> Commerce Clearing House
> 4025 West Peterson Avenue
> Chicago, Illinois   60646

Public Service Materials Center

PSMC (a commercial organization) publishes a series of books for grant-seekers, including:

Where America's Large Foundations Make Their Grants
Gives a select sampling of grants awarded by 750 foundations having at least $1 million in assets (Cost: $14.75).

The Survey of Grant-Making Foundations
Provides data on over 1,000 foundations with assets of $500,000 or more which give grants of over $25,000 (Cost: $7.95).

How to Get Your Fair Share of Foundation Grants
Overview of the foundation field, plus grant-winning suggestions by nine authorities (Cost: $12.00).

How to Raise Funds From Foundations
A how-to paperback covering approaches to foundations, proposal writing, and follow up (Cost: $8.95).

How to Write Successful Foundation Presentations
An 80-page paperback primer for grant-seekers on preparing letters, proposals, and renewal applications (Cost: $8.95).

In addition, PSMC also conducts seminars for nonprofessional grant-seekers.

For publication and seminar details write:

> Public Services Materials Center
> 355 Lexington Avenue
> New York, New York 10017

Seeking Foundation Funds

A 38-page guide written for the novice, *Seeking Foundation Funds,* outlines the foundation field and the basics of grant-seeking, from approach to formal application. Cost: $2.50.

To order, or for more information, write:

> National Public Relations Council
> 815 Second Avenue
> New York, New York 10017

Social Registers

Covering 13 major metropolitan locations, these directories provide personal and career data on thousands of prominent social leaders. Entries include: name and address, educational background, club, social and professional relationships.

The 13-city set covers: New York, Washington, Philadelphia, Chicago, Boston, St. Louis, Pittsburgh, Cleveland, Cincinnati, Dayton, San Francisco, Baltimore, and Buffalo. Directories can also be purchased separately. To order, or for more information, write:

> Social Register Association
> 381 Park Avenue South
> New York, New York 10016

The local directory is usually found in public or college libraries.

State Directories

A number of states publish directories of foundations, usually with full descriptions. For a free bibliography, write the Foundation Center, 888 Seventh Avenue, New York, New York 10019.

T & B Public Grants Services

Tamblyn & Brown, one of the largest full-service fundraising counseling firms in the world, is the parent organization of T & B Public Grants Services. This subsidiary counsels grant-seekers in both foundation and government fundraising.

For further information, write:

> Tamblyn & Brown, Inc.
> 350 Fifth Avenue
> New York, New York 10001

Taft Information System

The Taft Information System is a subsidiary of the financial management consulting firm of J. R. Taft Corporation. As part of its service, the Taft Information System researches the following materials, published by Taft Products:

Foundation Reporter—This annual paperback provides detailed information on some 250 major foundations:
> Name and type of foundation.
> Type, number, and geographical distribution of grants.
> Assets and total amounts of grants.
> Biographical data on officers, trustees, and whom to contact.
> Facts and analysis of the foundation's interests, restrictions, applications procedures, etc.
> Representative grant listings by category, with recipient name and grant amount.
> Five indexes: field of interest, foundations, foundations by state, foundation personnel, and grant types.

Foundation Reporter Supplement—Issued several times a year, primarily to update the *Foundation Reporter*.

News Monitor on Philanthropy—A monthly newsletter giving select grant data, plus news relevant to grant-seekers, such as personnel changes and upcoming conference dates.
Hot Line News—An occasionally issued bulletin alerting grant-seekers to vital late-breaking developments.

Cost for the complete service is $275. For further information write:

> J. R. Taft Corporation
> 1000 Vermont Avenue, N.W.
> Washington, D.C. 20005

In addition, Taft Products publishes a series of fund-raising books including *Proposal Writer's Swipe File,* a $5.50 paperback containing twelve sample proposals.

Telephone Directory

Don't overlook the telephone directory. Resourceful grant-seekers have sometimes used the directory to find the business number of a trustee not listed in the IRS Forms 990 and 990-AR.

Washington International Arts Letter

Published ten times a year, the *Washington International Arts Letter* provides detailed data on grants and other financial aid in the fields of art, the humanities, and education.

An annual subscription runs $16 for individuals, $32 for institutions.

WIAL also publishes several other aids to grant-seekers, including the book, *Private Foundations and Business Corporations Active in the Arts & Humanities/Education.* This

276-page paperback lists more than 6,000 representative grants made by over 1,000 foundations and almost 300 corporations for culturally related projects. Cost: $45.

For a subscription to the newsletter or a copy of the book, or for details on other publications, write:

> Washington International Arts Letter
> 1321 4th Street, S.W.
> Washington, D.C. 20024

Who's Who in America

A classic, this oversized two-volume directory is a rich source of biographical data on almost 70,000 leaders (including many foundation and corporate executives) in all fields and geographical locations.

Each brief sketch provides the grant-seeker with the following information: the individual's full name, position, personal and educational background. Other items include the person's business, political, club and religious affiliations, along with home and business addresses.

Copies of *Who's Who* are found in most public and college libraries. Regional and occupational editions are also published. For the current price and title lists write the publisher:

> A. N. Marquis Company
> 200 East Ohio Street
> Chicago, Illinois 60611

PART FOUR
Sample
Proposal

AUTHORS' NOTE   Each proposal is written to achieve its own purpose—not yours. As a result, reprinting an actual proposal would likely have been of limited value to you—unless you happened to have the identical project. Even then, times and circumstances change. For these reasons, we designed a model proposal on a universal subject: the high cost of rent. Keep in mind that our project is fictitious, as are the statistics, people, and organizations mentioned. Even the assumption that the IRS would allow the suggested tax deductions to building owners is open to debate. Our purpose was not to create an operative idea, but rather to give you an instructional vehicle illustrating many of the basic principles outlined in Part One, Step 8.

a proposal for a
$51,324 GRANT

to establish
A SERVICE TO LOCATE FREE OR LOW-COST
OFFICE SPACE FOR COMMUNITY SERVICE AGENCIES

submitted to
THE XYZ FOUNDATION

on
October 31, 1975

by
Dr. W. R. HELLERS
Executive Director
FRIENDS OF THE COMMUNITY, INC.
202 Park Avenue
New York, N.Y.   10017
(212) 618-0420

INTRODUCTION AND SUMMARY

This is a request to XYZ Foundation from Friends of the Community for a 1-year grant of $51,324 to establish Community Aid Real Estate Services (CARES).

CARES is needed because high rents are forcing many community service agencies to curtail their activities. CARES will persuade building owners to donate idle space to community-service agencies for free or at a low cost. In exchange, the building owners will receive tax-deduction benefits.

Exactly $20,580 has been pledged by local business firms and individuals towards CARES' first-year operating budget of $71,904. This leaves $51,324 to be raised, the amount we are requesting from you.

CARES' first year of operation will be supervised by Friends of the Community, a tax-exempt organization founded in 1946. Our membership comprises 47 distinguished community leaders. We are the only organization in New York that fosters new community service agencies—and our success stories are many.

THE NEED

An increasing number of community service agencies are being forced to restrict their programs—or to cease their operations entirely—because escalating rents absorb too much of their operating budgets. And many have had to turn away volunteer office workers because they can't afford to expand their facilities.[1]

At the same time, much office space lies idle. The occupancy rate of New York City office buildings averages 90 percent, which means that approximately 25,000,000 square feet of space remain unrented. Of this space, more than 5,000,000 square feet have been idle for at least a year. Result: loss of significant income for the building owners.[2]

---

1. See Addendum for a detailed description of these community-service agencies and for letters from community-service agencies verifying the need.
2. See Addendum for a letter from the Gotham Real Estate Board verifying these facts.

If a real-estate firm allowed a nonprofit organization to use its idle space free, or at a reduced rate, then the firm would benefit from a tax saving.[3]

Therefore, if building owners and nonprofit organizations could coordinate their needs, both would benefit. Yet there is no system to match up the city's 2,500 office-building owners with the hundreds of space-needing nonprofit organizations. Nor is there any realistic funding source outside of a foundation to finance the establishment of such a system.[4]

THE OBJECTIVE

Friends of the Community seeks to create an independent nonprofit agency called CARES to help nonprofit community agencies locate free or low-cost office space in New York. CARES' long-range objective is to encourage the establishment of similar programs in other cities.

THE METHODS

JANUARY—Hire the staff: Executive Director, Assistant Director and secretary. Set up the office (lease, furniture, stationery, etc.). Prepare and print a descriptive brochure. We recognize that building CARES' credibility and awareness within the real-estate industry is vital. Therefore, we will initiate a PR campaign by mailing the brochure to real-estate-industry leaders, by sending news releases to the trade and general media, and by making a speech at the Gotham Real Estate Club.

FEBRUARY (first half)—The staff will identify and contact the best building-owner prospects by interviewing real-estate-industry leaders and bank officers. CARES will emphasize the tax-saving benefits to the prospects. Data sheets on the available space will be prepared.

FEBRUARY (second half)—CARES will inform the community service agency of its new program through meetings, mailings, telephone

3. See Addendum for the IRS ruling on this type of tax deduction and for a tax lawyer's interpretation of this ruling.
4. See Addendum for a list of government officials and real-estate authorities who can verify these assertions.

calls, and publicity. Data sheets on the space needs will be prepared.

MARCH—Using the data sheets, CARES will look for logical matchups between the space-seekers and space-donors. Whenever one occurs, CARES will bring the two parties together.

APRIL THROUGH DECEMBER—The staff will continue to operate and expand the program. Potential pitfall: fading from the real-estate-industry's spotlight. Therefore CARES will maintain a strong PR program.

YEAR TWO—CARES will become self-supporting (see "The Program's Future" section). CARES will make its success story and procedures known to other cities through brochures and publicity.

ORGANIZATION QUALIFICATIONS

Friends of the Community is a tax-exempt 501 (C) (3) nonprofit organization[5] founded in 1946. Membership comprises 47 metropolitan leaders from a cross-section of business and professional fields. Our sole purpose is to help the city by fostering new community-service agencies which have the capacity to become self-supporting within a year or two. Some of our better-known successes are The Museum Visiting Program for Children, The Community Day-Care Training Center, The Senior Citizen's Education Center, and Camp Holiwak (for handicapped children).

CARES' Executive Director will be Marion Towne, whose experience includes: Vice President of ACME Real Estate Corporation (1970 to present) and Director of Public Relations of the Empire Life Insurance Corporation (1966 to 1970)[6]. The Assistant Director is yet to be selected, but finding a qualified person should pose no problem because of Marion Towne's broad contacts in the real-estate feld.

The following community leaders have agreed to serve on the Board of Trustees of CARES: Allen Burns (former Executive Director of the Greater New York Charity League), Carole Grenoble (President of Grenoble & Grenoble Real Estate Brokers and past Presi-

---

5. See Addendum for 501 (C) (3) photocopy.
6. See Addendum for resumé of Marion Towne.

dent of the Gotham Real Estate Club), Herbert Henshaw (Executive Vice President of Real Estate of the Metro Bank), Joseph Materi (Chairman of the Board of Wide World Consolidated Insurance Corporation), and Norma Pascade (Senior Partner of the law firm Cello & Checker).

THE EVALUATION

We believe it is reasonable to assume that the project will be a success if the value of the donated office space is at least ten times the cost of the program. In other words, if CARES' operating budget is $6,000 per month, CARES should save community-service agencies at least $60,000 a month in rent.

CARES plans to reach the 10:1 ratio before the end of its first fiscal year. T. R. Jones, Senior Vice President of Real Estate of the Gotham National Bank, has agreed to estimate each month the value of the office space generated by CARES.

Reporting procedure: CARES will furnish you with interim reports quarterly (March 31, June 30, and September 30) and a more detailed final report on December 31. T. R. Jones's impartial estimates will be included in each report.

BUDGET

Note: This budget covers the first year of operation. Some of the operating expenses have already been donated or committed (indicated by asterisks). See the Addendum for the list of givers.

		TOTALS
PERSONNEL:		
Executive Director @ $1500 per month (full time)		$18,000
Assistant to the Executive Director @ $900 per month (full time)		$10,800
Secretary @ $700 per month (full time)		$8,400
Payroll expenses (FICA taxes, insurance, etc.) @ 10 percent of salaries		$3,720
SUBTOTAL: PERSONNEL		$40,920

OUTSIDE SERVICES:

Bookkeeping @ $100 per month	$1,200	
Legal services @ $200 per month	$2,400*	
Public relations counseling services @ $200 per month	$2,400*	
Program-evaluation services @ $200 per month	$2,400*	
SUBTOTAL: OUTSIDE SERVICES		$8,400

RENT:

One thousand square feet @ $8 per year	$8,000*	$8,000

UTILITIES:

Three telephones @ $10 per month each	$360	
Telephone installation charge	$50	
Local message units: 500 calls per month @ 10c	$600	
Long-distance calls @ $50 per month	$600	
Gas & electric (part of rent)	$0	
SUBTOTAL: UTILITIES		$1,610

EQUIPMENT:

Two typewriters @ $20 per month rental each	$480*	
Adding machine (to be purchased)	$100	
Multi-copy machine @ $40 per month rental	$480	
Furniture and furnishings (desks, chairs, file cabinets, etc.)	$3,000*	
SUBTOTAL: EQUIPMENT		$4,060

SUPPLIES:

Printed stationery and forms	$400*	
Postage stamps @ $50 per month	$600	
Multi-copy paper @ $30 per month	$360	
General office supplies @ $50 per month	$600	
SUBTOTAL: SUPPLIES		$1,960

TRAVEL AND MEETINGS:

Local transportation (subway, taxi, etc.) @ $100 per month	$1,200	
Executive Director's trip to Boston for the National Community Service Conference ($60 airfare, $25 ground		

transportation, $45 registration fee,
$60 for two days' lodging and $40 for
two days' per diem) $230

SUBTOTAL: TRAVEL AND MEETINGS $1,430

MISCELLANEOUS EXPENSES:
Preparation and printing of 10,000 copies
  of a 16-page brochure describing CARES
  @ 15c $1,500*
Reference library (books, trade magazines,
  etc.) $300
Property and liability insurance $300

SUBTOTAL: MISCELLANEOUS EXPENSES $2,100

GENERAL RESERVE:
@ 5 percent of itemized budget (to be used for
  contingencies) $3,424

GRAND TOTAL:
Total budget $71,904

Less funds already donated or committed
  (indicated above with an asterisk) $20,580

FUNDS STILL NEEDED: $51,324

THE PROGRAM'S FUTURE

Starting in year two, CARES will charge community service agencies a fee equal to 10 percent of the fair market value of the donated office space. (In year one, the service will be free in order to get the program rolling.) The 10 percent fee generated by the project should be more than ample to cover basic operating expenses. Surplus will be used to expand and refine the service locally and to encourage the establishment of similar programs in other cities.

Appendixes

APPENDIX A

History and Trends

Foundation lineage dates back to the Golden Age of Greece, but the foundation entity as we know it today is basically a twentieth-century American phenomenon. Even other industrial nations, such as Japan and Germany, are modeling their foundation institutions after ours.

The American foundation dollar represents about 8 percent of the some $25 billion contributions made each year by the private sector of our economy. In 1974, according to the American Association of Fund-Raising Counsel, the remainder came from living individuals (79 percent), bequests (8 percent), and corporations (5 percent). In addition, approximately 500 government agencies dispersed some $50 billion for philanthropic and quasi-philanthropic activities.

The Tax Reform Act of 1969

The American foundation field grew relatively unbridled until 1969, the year that Congress enacted its now-famous Tax Reform Act. Since then foundations have been required to operate under a strict set of laws.

The foundation portion of the Tax Reform Act of 1969 was precipitated mainly by the abuses of self-serving foundations. These wrongdoings took many forms. For instance, unethical foundations paid family members exorbitant salaries, loaned their donors money at negligible interest rates, and used their economic power to help the donors' businesses.

These self-dealing practices gave the entire foundation field a black eye and led one U.S. Senator to comment, "Too many foundations are the playthings of the rich." But the truth of the matter was that only a minute percentage of all foundations were guilty of self-dealing. The rest conducted their philanthropic operations scrupulously. Today, these well-behaved foundations are paying for the sins of their wayward siblings through special taxes and stricter regulations. To illustrate: a foundation must now:

Pay a 4 percent (subject to legislative change) excise tax on its net investment income.

Distribute in grants at least 6 percent of its assets each year (subject to exceptions).

Submit detailed reports on how its grant dollars are being used.

Own no more than 20 percent of any corporation's voting shares.

Make no investment that would endanger its assets.

If these and other strictures of the Tax Reform Act of 1969 are violated, then both the foundation and its officials face stiff IRS penalties. This threat has caused many nonprofessionally staffed foundations to be more conservative in choosing their grantees. Also a number of smaller foundations have elected to go out of business rather than face the increased paperwork or risk the harsh IRS penalties.

Yet the Tax Reform Act of 1969 (and its subsequent revisions) has worked for the benefit of grant-seekers. The reporting procedures furnish grant-aspirants with specific data on the foundation's assets, officers, trustees, and grant recipients. Few foundations made this information available to the public prior to the Tax Reform Act of 1969.

Trends

No foundation watcher can predict the future with any certainty, but the informed consensus forecasts a number of likely trends:

First, there will be increased professionalism in foundation management, a result of the Tax Reform Act of 1969. And some foundations will attempt to minimize their legal risk by specializing in fewer areas and by relying more heavily on the opinions of outside experts.

The Act will probably reduce the number of foundations, but not the total number of foundation dollars, a sum expected to parallel the Gross National Product.

The distribution of foundation dollars will almost certainly change, but predicting which fields will receive more or less would be only a blind guess. Too many variables are involved, including changing public needs and the fashionability of causes.

The number of grant-seekers will probably rise and, by and large, they will be more sophisticated in their grant searches. All this will result in stronger competition for each available grant dollar.

APPENDIX B

The Most-Funded Fields

What are the most-funded fields? The breakdown for the grants appearing in the 1973 *Foundation Grants Index* was:

    36 percent for education
    24 percent for health
    12 percent for science and technology
     9 percent for welfare
     9 percent for international activities
     8 percent for humanities
     2 percent for religion

The breakdown within each of the above six fields was:

EDUCATION

37 percent for endowment
19 percent for higher education
10 percent for buildings and equipment
6 percent for educational research
6 percent for elementary and secondary education
5 percent for communications
4 percent for libraries
4 percent for personnel development
3 percent for scholarships and loans
2 percent for fellowships
2 percent for educational associations
1 percent for adult education
1 percent for vocational education

HEALTH

34 percent for medical
   education
26 percent for hospitals
15 percent for public health
13 percent for medical care &
   rehabilitation

6 percent for dentistry
3 percent for mental health
2 percent for nursing
1 percent for health agencies

SCIENCE AND TECHNOLOGY

27 percent for medical research
10 percent for environmental
   studies
10 percent for law
 7 percent for earth sciences &
   oceanography
 7 percent for political science
 7 percent for psychology
 6 percent for business & labor
 5 percent for sociology
 5 percent for technology
 3 percent for chemistry
 3 percent for economics

3 percent for social sciences
   (general)
2 percent for agriculture
2 percent for biology
1 percent for mathematics
1 percent for physics
1 percent for miscellaneous
   sub-categories: anthro-
   pology, archaeology,
   astronomy and space,
   physical sciences in
   general, and sciences in
   general

WELFARE

21 percent for community
   development
21 percent for youth agencies
13 percent for child welfare
10 percent for community
   funds
 8 percent for race relations
 6 percent for social agencies

5 percent for handicapped
5 percent for recreation and
   conservation
4 percent for delinquency and
   crime
4 percent for housing and
   transportation
3 percent for aged

INTERNATIONAL ACTIVITIES

30 percent for education
25 percent for health and
   welfare
23 percent for technical
   assistance
13 percent for international
   studies

3 percent for cultural
   relations
3 percent for peace and international cooperation
2 percent for exchange of
   persons
1 percent for relief and
   refugees

HUMANITIES

33 percent for performing arts
   (general)
28 percent for museums
15 percent for music
 8 percent for humanities
   (general)

8 percent for art and
   architecture
5 percent for history
2 percent for language and
   literature
1 percent for philosophy

RELIGION

41 percent for theological
   education
27 percent for religious welfare
17 percent for religious
   associations
 6 percent for theology
 4 percent for buildings and
   equipment

3 percent for churches and
   temples
1 percent for religious
   education
1 percent for religion
   (general)

The above statistics have four primary limitations. First, their universe is restricted to grants of $5,000 or more recorded by the Foundation Center. Second, a single $60-million grant for an "Education Endowment" made that particular sub-field total abnormally large. Third, a grant may logically fit into two fields, but can be listed only in one.

Fourth, the relative share of each field and sub-field varies from year to year. Often a field becomes temporarily "fashionable" and then fades from the center spotlight, as was the case with funding for American Indian causes a decade ago. Significant fluctuations also occur in the "staple" fields. For instance, the education field's share seesawed from 24 percent to 46 percent over a ten-year time span.

Yet the Foundation Center statistics are by far the best available, and they do give a reasonable approximation of how foundation dollars are distributed among the various fields and sub-fields.

APPENDIX C

Government Agencies

Although there are some similarities between a foundation and a government grant, the latter is a horse of a different color. To describe the ins and outs of government grant-seeking requires a book in itself. As a matter of fact, we are considering writing one as a companion to this volume.

The purpose of Appendix C is to direct you to the key government publications in the event that you are seeking a government grant.

Catalog of Federal Domestic Assistance—This massive annual tome lists and describes practically all federal programs and activities that socially or economically aid the public. It details the assistance provided by almost 900 agencies, commissions, and councils, including grants, loans and loan guarantees, scholarships, training, technical aid, statistical data, equipment, and facilities. A new edition comes out during early summer and may be purchased for $14.50 plus $2.50 for the binder. (The supplement is free.) For your copy of the *Catalog,* visit your local Federal Book Store, or write:

Superintendent of Documents
U.S. Government Printing Office
Washington, D.C. 20402

Federal Register—This daily periodical gives you advance notice of the programs, eligibility requirements, application procedures, and other relevant data on forthcoming and renewed grant-making programs of the various federal agencies. An annual subscription runs $45 and includes a monthly index. A single month's subscription costs $5 while a single issue runs 75¢. The monthly index can be ordered separately for $8 per year. For your *Federal Register* subscription write the Superintendent of Documents.

Department of Health, Education and Welfare—This super-agency is by far the biggest source of dollars distributed to public causes. For free descriptive literature on programs and activities relating to your specific field of interest write:

Office of the Secretary
DHEW
Washington, D.C. 20201

Quasi-Governmental Agencies—There are three well-endowed agencies directly supported by annual appropriations from Congress, but which operate independently of government control. Each publishes a detailed document providing descriptions of its grant-making policies and its application procedures:

National Endowment for the Arts—The *Guide to Programs* published by the Endowment covers its key program areas: Architecture and Environmental Arts; Dance; Education;

Expansion Arts; Federal-State Partnership; Literature; Museums; Music; Public Media; Special Projects; Theatre; Visual Arts. For a free copy of the *Guide* write:

> Public Information Officer
> National Endowment for the Arts
> Washington, D.C. 20506

National Endowment for the Humanities—A *Program Announcement* booklet provides information on the Endowment's five programs: Education, Public, Research Grants, Fellowships and Stipends, Youthgrants in the Humanities. For a free copy write:

> Public Information Officer
> National Endowment for the Humanities
> Washington, D.C. 20506

National Science Foundation—The Foundation funds scientific research and educational projects in the mathematical, physical, medical, biological, social, and engineering sciences. For a free copy of a "Guide to Programs" booklet write:

> Public Affairs Office
> National Science Foundation
> Washington, D.C. 20550

APPENDIX D

Scholarship Funds

As with government grants, scholarships and advanced study awards are beyond the scope of this book. However, we felt it necessary at least to direct you to the leading sources of information.

Your college's student-aid office is usually the best source of information because:

Scholarship funds are in a constant state of flux. New scholarships appear from nowhere, while old ones dry up. Only a student-aid office can keep abreast of these changes.

The vast majority of scholarship funds are local in scope, and therefore, are seldom listed in the national directories.

Of the national directories, two are especially useful. Both are primarily designed for fund-seeking individuals as opposed to organizations. Each contains a variety of funding listings: grants, scholarships, advanced study awards. Funding sources include government agencies, businesses, associations, fraternal organizations, and foundations. You can probably find them in your local public or college library:

Annual Register of Grant Support—674 pages. $47.50 hardcover. Published by Marquis Who's Who, Inc., 4300 West 62 Street, Indianapolis, Indiana 46268.

Grants Register—800 pages. $17.50 hardcover. Published by St. Martin's Press, 175 Fifth Avenue, New York, N.Y. 10010. The geographical scope of this book is broad: all English-speaking countries.

In addition, there are paperback books dealing with scholarships and advanced study awards. You can find them for sale in bookstores, especially those located on or near campuses.

APPENDIX E

IRS Form 990-AR Sample

Form 990—AR

1974
Annual Report
of Private
Foundation

Name

Under Section 6056 of the Internal Revenue Code

In addition to this Annual Report,
the annual return of the Foundation
filed on Form 990—PF is available for
public inspection. Consult an
Internal Revenue Service office for
further information.

Department
of the
Treasury
Internal
Revenue
Service

Form 990–AR

Annual report for calendar year 1971

Name of organization	Employer identification number
OLIN FOUNDATION, INC.	13-1820176

Address of principal office

99 Park Avenue, New York, New York 10016

If books and records are not at above address, specify where they are kept	Name of principal officer of foundation
2700 Foshay Tower, Minneapolis, Minnesota 55402	Charles L. Horn, President

Revenues

1 Amount of gifts, grants, bequests, and contributions received for the year	None
2 Gross income for the year	3,109,750.27
3 Total.	3,109,750.27

Disbursements and Expenses

Grants $4,956,353.13+Expenses for which exempt $102,476.63

4 Disbursements for the year for the purposes for which exempt (including administrative expenses) .	5,058,829.76
5 Expenses attributable to gross income (item 2 above) for the year (From Form 990) .	216,442.61

Foundation Managers

6 List all managers of the foundation (see section 4946(b) IRC):

Name and title	Address where manager may be contacted during normal business hours
Charles L. Horn - President	2700 Foshay Tower, Minneapolis, Minnesota
James O. Wynn - Vice President	99 Park Avenue, New York, New York
Ralph Clark - Secretary- Treasurer	33 North Dearborn St., Chicago, Illinois
C.T. Helming - Assistant Secretary	2700 Foshay Tower, Minneapolis, Minnesota

6a List here any managers of the foundation (see section 4946(b) IRC; who have contributed 2 percent of the total contributions received by the foundation before the close of any taxable year (but only if they have contributed more than $5,000). (See section 507(d)(2).)

NONE

6b List here any managers of the foundation (see section 4946(b) IRC; who own 10 percent or more of the stock of a corporation (or an equally large portion of the ownership of a partnership or other entity) of which the foundation has a 10 percent or greater interest.

NONE

181

Balance Sheet Per Books at the Beginning of the Year

Assets			Liabilities	
Cash		802,177	Accounts payable	130,854
Certificates of Deposit		3,800,000	Contributions, gifts, grants, etc. payable	
Accounts and notes receivable . . .				
Inventories			Bonds and notes payable	
Securities		6,096,491	Mortgages payable	
Government obligations				
Corporate bonds		14,803,041	Other liabilities	
Corporate stocks		19,598,845	Total liabilities	
			Net Worth	
Mortgage loans			Principal fund	44,576,140
Real estate				
Less: Depreciation .			Income fund	394,360
Other assets . . .	800			
Less: Depreciation .		800	Total net worth	44,970,500
Total assets		45,101,354	Total liabilities and net worth . . .	45,101,354

Itemized Statement of Securities and All Other Assets Held at the Close of the Taxable Year

Asset	Book value	Market value
Cash	647,376	647,376
Certificates of Deposit	6,300,000	6,300,000
U.S. Treasury Bills	3,362,487	3,362,487
U.S. Treasury Bonds	503,938	503,938
Federal National Mortgage Assoc. Bonds	74,719	74,719
Non-Governmental Bonds (List Attached)	14,603,041	11,526,003
Corporate Stocks (List Attached)	19,048,580	71,239,570
Travel Advances	800	800
Total	44,540,941	93,654,893

Grants and Contributions Paid or Approved for Future Payment During the Year

Recipient Name and address (home or business)	If recipient is an individual, show any relationship to any foundation manager or substantial contributor	Concise statement of purpose of grant or contribution	Amount
Paid during year			
Total			
Approved for future payment			
Total			

A notice has been published that this Annual Report is available for public inspection at the principal offices of the foundation, and copies of this Annual Report have been furnished to the Attorney of each State entitled to receive reports as required by instruction "F."

Date	Signature of foundation manager		Title

Date	Signature of individual or firm preparing the report	Preparer's address	Emp. Ident. or Soc. Sec. No.

Instructions

A. Annual Report.—An annual report is required from the foundation managers (as defined in section 4946(b)) of every organization which is a private foundation, including a trust described in section 4947(a)(1) which is treated as a private foundation, having at least $5,000 of assets at any time during a taxable year. A private foundation may use this form for its annual reporting requirements.

If you prefer not to use this form, you may prepare the annual report in printed, typewritten or any other form you choose, provided it readily and legibly discloses the information required by section 6056 and the regulations thereunder.

The annual report is in addition to and not in lieu of submitting the information required on Form 990-PF under section 6033.

B. Where and When to File.—The annual report must be filed at the time and place specified for filing Form 990-PF.

C. Public Inspection of Private Foundation's Annual Reports.—As a foundation manager, you must make the annual report required by section 6056 available at the principal office of the foundation for inspection during regular business hours by any citizen who so requests within 180 days after publication of notice of its availability; or, if you choose, you may furnish a copy free of charge to such persons requesting inspection, provided these persons do so at the time and manner prescribed in section 6104(d) and the regulations thereunder.

The notice must be published not later than the day prescribed for filing the annual report (determined with regard to any extensions of time for filing), in a newspaper having general circulation in the county in which the principal office of the private foundation is located. The notice must state that the annual report of the private foundation is available at its principal office during regular business hours for inspection by any citizen who so requests within 180 days after the date of the

publication. It must also show the address of the private foundation's principal office and the name of its principal manager. A private foundation may designate in addition to its principal office, or (if the foundation has no principal office or none other than the residence of a substantial contributor or foundation manager) instead of such office, any other location where its annual report is available.

The term "newspaper having general circulation" shall include any newspaper or journal which is permitted to publish statements in satisfaction of State statutory requirements relating to transfer of title to real estate or other similar legal notices.

A copy of the notice must be attached to the annual report filed with the Internal Revenue Service.

A private foundation which has terminated its status as such under section 507(b)(1)(A), by distributing all its net assets to one or more public charities without retaining any right, title or interest in such assets, does not have to publish notice of availability of its annual report or furnish such report to the public for the taxable year in which it so terminates (Reg. 1.507–2(a)(6)).

D. Signature and Verification.—The report must be signed by the foundation manager.

E. List of States.—A private foundation is required to attach to its Form 990-PF a list of all States:

(a) to which the organization reports in any fashion concerning its organization, assets, or activities, and

(b) with which the organization has registered (or which it has otherwise notified in any manner) that it intends to be, or is a charitable organization or that it is, or intends to be, a holder of property devoted to a charitable purpose.

F. Furnishing of Copies to State Officers; Listing of States.—The foundation managers must furnish a copy of the annual report (required by section 6056) to the Attorney Gen-

eral of (1) each State listed for Form 990-PF above, (2) the State in which the principal office of the foundation is located, and (3) the State in which the foundation was incorporated or organized. Such report must be furnished at the same time it is sent to the Internal Revenue Service. In addition, the foundation managers shall provide upon request a copy of the annual report to the Attorney General or other appropriate State officer of any other State. The foundation manager shall also attach to the report a copy of the Form 990-PF (or Schedule PF (Form 1041) for a 4947(a)(1) trust) and a copy of the Form 4720 (if any) filed by the foundation with the Internal Revenue Service for the year.

G. Penalty for Failure to File Report and Notice on Time.—If a private foundation fails to file the annual report on or before the due date, or to comply with the requirements under "C" above, there will be imposed on the person (anyone under a duty to perform the act), a $10 penalty for each day during which the failure continues, not to exceed $5,000. (See section 6652(d)(3).) If more than one person is liable, all such persons shall be jointly and severally liable with respect to such failure. Organizations that have given notice under section 508(b) as to their status and have not received a letter from the Internal Revenue Service containing a determination as to such status—refer to Revenue Procedure 72–31, 1972–1 C.B. 759, or later revisions, for rules relating to relief from the penalty provision of Section 6652. If the failure to file the annual report or comply with "C" is willful, there will be imposed, in addition to the amount mentioned above, a penalty of $1,000 for each such report or notice. (See section 6685.)

H. Foreign Organizations.—A foreign organization which has received substantially all of its support (other than gross investment income) from sources outside the United States will not be subject to the requirements of instructions "C" and "F" above.

☆ U.S. GOVERNMENT PRINTING OFFICE : 1974—O-548-036

CLIN FOUNDATION, INC.

Calendar Year 1971

Schedule of Contributions, gifts, grants and similar amounts paid for
Part II, Line 9, Form 990 and Form 990-AR

Name of Grantee	Purpose	Amount
Case Western Reserve University Cleveland, Ohio	Crawford Building Computer Center Construction	$1,000,000.00
Clemson University Clemson, South Carolina	Student Loan & Scholarship Fund	100,00.00
Colgate University Hamilton, New York	Life Science Building Construction	322,302.34
Jarvis Christian College Hawkins, Texas	Science Building Construction Books	3,356.40 76.19
Macalester College St. Paul, Minnesota	Harvey M. Rice Building Construction	105,226.05
University of Southern California Los Angeles, California	Communication Center Construction	825,500.00
Vanderbilt University Nashville, Tennessee	Chemical Engineering Building Construction	840,960.27
Whitman College Walla Walla, Washington	Science Building Construction	1,758,931.88

$4,956,353.13

During 1971, the above specific and unconditional grants were made to
defray the cost of constructing and equipping certain buildings and
facilities for qualified educational institutions.

184

APPENDIX F

Applying for Tax-Exempt Status

To receive tax-exempt status, you must first become a non-profit corporation performing one of the IRS sanctioned activities. In simple terms, these fundable areas are charitable, educational, religious, scientific, and cultural.

Application approval takes anywhere from two weeks to two years, depending on several variables: your lawyer's expertise, the IRS backlog, your organization record, your field of interest—and luck. Once approved, you're officially designated as a 501 (C) (3) tax-exempt organization and receive the IRS Letter of Exemption.

You can file the application yourself, but the use of a qualified lawyer usually proves best in the long run. Expect to pay anywhere from $50 to $300 for this legal assistance.

For the proper application form, write your local IRS office, or write to:

> Commissioner
> Internal Revenue Bureau
> 1111 Constitution Avenue
> Washington, D.C.   20224

Ask for IRS Form 1023 (the application form for applying for IRS 501 (C) (3) status) plus IRS Publication 557 (the detailed instructions on determining your eligibility).

Also check with your State Attorney General's office for regulations that might affect you.

Bibliography

In the previous pages we have mentioned a number of how-to books. In addition, there are a number of books that will give the serious foundation student an excellent background understanding of the foundation field. Here is a select list:

The Big Foundations by Waldemar A. Nielsen (Columbia University Press, New York, 1972, 475 pages).

English Philanthropy, 1660–1960 by David Owen (Harvard University Press, Cambridge, 1964, 610 pages).

The Foundation Administrator: A Study of Those Who Manage America's Foundations by Arnold J. Zurcher and Jane Dustan (Russell Sage Foundation, New York, 1972, 171 pages).

Foundations, Private Giving and Public Policy by the Commission on Foundations and Private Philanthropy (University of Chicago Press, Chicago, 1970, 287 pages).

Foundations: 20 Viewpoints edited by F. Emerson Andrews (Russell Sage Foundation, New York, 1965, 108 pages).

Foundations Under Fire edited by Thomas C. Reeves (Cornell University Press, Ithaca, 1970, 235 pages).

Foundation Watcher by F. Emerson Andrews (Franklin and Marshall College, Lancaster, Pa., 1973, 321 pages).

The Future of Foundations edited by Fritz R. Heimann (The American Assembly, distributed by Prentice-Hall, Inc., Englewood Cliffs, N.J., 1973, 278 pages).

Guide to European Foundations compiled by the Giovanni Agnelli Foundation (Columbia University Press, New York, 1973, 401 pages).

The Investment Policies of Foundations by Ralph L. Nelson (Russell Sage Foundation, New York, 1967, 203 pages).

Management of American Foundations: Administration, Policies and Social Role by Arnold J. Zurcher (New York University Press, New York, 1972, 184 pages).

The Money Givers by Joseph C. Goulden (Random House, New York, 1971, 341 pages).

Operating Principles of the Larger Foundations by Joseph C. Kiger (Russell Sage Foundation, New York, 1954, 151 pages).

Philanthropic Foundations by F. Emerson Andrews (Russell Sage Foundation, New York, 1956, 459 pages).

Philanthropy in England, 1480–1660 by W. K. Jordan (Russell Sage Foundation, New York, 1959, 410 pages).

Private Money and Public Service: The Role of Foundations in American Society by Merrimon Cuninggim (McGraw-Hill, New York, 1972, 267 pages).

Public Information Handbook for Foundations by Saul Richman (Council on Foundations, New York, 1973, 95 pages).

Understanding Foundations by J. R. Taft (McGraw-Hill, New York, 1967, 205 pages).

U.S. Philanthropic Foundations: Their History, Structure, Management, and Record by Warren Weaver (Harper & Row, New York, 1967, 492 pages).